Elements of Crisis Intervention

Elements of Crisis Intervention

Crises and How to Respond to Them

Third Edition

James L. Greenstone
Diplomate, American Board of Examiners in Crisis Intervention,
Police Psychologist, City of Fort Worth, Texas Police Department
(Retired)

Sharon C. Leviton
Diplomate, American Board of Examiners in Crisis Intervention

BROOKS/COLE
CENGAGE Learning™

Australia • Canada • Mexico • Singapore • Spain • United Kingdom • United States

BROOKS/COLE
CENGAGE Learning™

Elements of Crisis Intervention: Crises and How to Respond to Them, Third Edition

James L. Greenstone, Sharon C. Leviton

Publisher/Executive Editor: Linda Schreiber-Ganster

Acquisitions Editor: Seth Dobrin

Editorial Assistant: Suzanna Kincaid

Marketing Manager: Trent Whatcott

Marketing Coordinator: Gurpreet Saran

Marketing Communications Manager: Tami Strang

Content Project Management: PreMediaGlobal

Art Director: Caryl Gorska

Print Buyer: Linda Hsu

Manufacturing Manager: Marcia Locke

Rights Acquisition Director: Bob Kauser

Rights Acquisition Specialist, Text/Image: Roberta Broyer

Production Service/Compositor: PreMediaGlobal

Cover Designer: Jeremy, Mende Design

Cover Image: Mende Design

For product information and technology assistance, contact us at **Cengage Learning Customer & Sales Support, 1-800-354-9706**

For permission to use material from this text or product, submit all requests online at **www.cengage.com/permissions.**

Further permissions questions can be emailed to **permissionrequest@cengage.com.**

Library of Congress Control Number: 2010933627

ISBN-13: 978-0-495-00781-4

ISBN-10: 0-495-00781-1

Brooks-Cole
20 Davis Drive
Belmont, CA 94002-3098
USA

Cengage Learning is a leading provider of customized learning solutions with office locations around the globe, including Singapore, the United Kingdom, Australia, Mexico, Brazil, and Japan. Locate your local office at **www.cengage.com/global.**

Cengage Learning products are represented in Canada by Nelson Education, Ltd.

For your course and learning solutions, visit **www.cengage.com.**

Purchase any of our products at your local college store or at our preferred online store **www.cengagebrain.com.**

Printed in the United States of America
1 2 3 4 5 6 7 14 13 12 11 10

We dedicate this book to our colleagues Edward S. Rosenbluh, Ph.D. (1937–2000); W. Rodney Fowler, Ed.D.; Kent A. Rensin, Ph.D.; and Lieutenant of Police James E. Oney, pioneers in the field of Crisis Management. Over the years we have taught alongside them, and we continue to learn from them.

We honor the life of Rosalie Palter Cohen (1910–2010), whose resilient spirit never wavered. Her belief that effective intervention could assist a person not only to endure but also to prevail will continue to inspire us.

About the Authors

JAMES GREENSTONE

Dr. Greenstone is in private clinical and forensic practice. For over ten years he served as Police Psychologist and Director of the Psychological Services Unit of the Fort Worth Police Department.

Prior to his retirement from the Department he developed, organized, trained, and supervised the department's Peer Support Team. He has trained peer teams for other police agencies and for the federal government, including the United States Border Patrol. At Fort Worth P.D., he was Coordinator of the Critical Incident Stress Management program and a member and trainer of the department's Hostage and Crisis Negotiation Team. He has been in practice for 45 years, and has been a police officer for over 35 years. Previously, he served with the Dallas County Sheriff's Department, with the Lancaster, Texas Police Department, the Fort Worth Police Department and with the Tarrant County Sheriff's Department. He is certified as a Master Peace Officer, as a Mental Health Peace Officer, and as a Forensic Hypnotist by the Texas Commission on Law Enforcement Officer Standards and Education. He holds police instructor certificates from Texas and several other states. Currently, he is a deputy Constable and Police Behavioral Health Specialist with the Tarrant County Constable's Office, Precinct 4. Formerly, he was Adjunct Professor of Law at the Texas Wesleyan University School of Law and was Lead Hostage and Crisis Negotiations Instructor at the North Central Texas Council of Governments Regional Police Academy. He is a licensed professional counselor, a licensed marriage and family therapist, and a dispute mediator and arbitrator. He holds earned degrees in Clinical Psychology, Education, Criminal Justice, and Law. He interned at the Devereux Foundation in Devon, Pennsylvania.

Dr. Greenstone is a member of the graduate faculties at Walden University and Capella University, and formerly was with the University of Phoenix. His appointments include both Clinical and Forensic Psychology, and Criminal Justice.

Dr. Greenstone is Editor-in-Chief Emeritus of the *Journal of Police Crisis Negotiations,* an international journal published by Taylor and Francis Group under the Routledge brand. Dr. Greenstone also edited the *Journal of Crisis Negotiations* and the *International Journal of Police Negotiations and Crisis Management.* These journals were the predecessors of the current publication. Previously, he was Editor-in-Chief of *Emotional First Aid: A Journal of Crisis Intervention.*

Dr. Greenstone is a Diplomate in Crisis Intervention from the American Board of Examiners in Crisis Intervention and served as Chairman of that body; a Diplomate in Police Psychology from the Society for Police and Criminal Psychology; a Diplomate in Traumatic Stress from the American Academy of Experts in Traumatic Stress; and a Fellow of the College of the American College of Forensic Examiners. He is a practitioner member of the Academy of Family Mediators/ Association for Conflict Resolution, and is a Certified Traumatologist.

Dr. Greenstone is the author of *Elements of Police Hostage and Crisis Negotiations: Critical Incidents and How to Respond to Them,* published by Haworth Press, Inc., in 2005. He is the author of multiple other works in the fields of Crisis Intervention and Dispute Mediation. His most recent work, *The Elements of Disaster Psychology: Managing Psychosocial Trauma,* was published in 2008 by Charles C. Thomas, Publisher.

SHARON LEVITON

Dr. Leviton holds degrees in Education and Crisis Intervention, and is a crisis specialist and a dispute mediator in private practice in Fort Worth, Texas. Formerly, she was an adjunct professor of law at the Texas Wesleyan University School of Law, and an individual and family psychotherapist. She has been in practice for 35 years.

Dr. Leviton served as Executive Director for the Southwestern Academy of Crisis Interveners; served on the board of the American Academy of Crisis Interveners; and was Associate Director of the National Training Conference for Crisis Intervention and a faculty member of the National Institute on Training in Crisis Intervention.

Dr. Leviton has authored books, articles, papers, training manuals, and editorials in the fields of psychotherapy, Crisis Intervention, stress management, dispute resolution, and crisis communications. She has lectured and presented workshops nationally and internationally. She was appointed by the Fort Worth City Council to the Disciplinary Appeals Board.

Brief Contents

Contents

In addition to listing the areas covered in the chapters, this table of contents is a step-by-step guide to the intervention process and should be used by interveners to guide an intervention in an orderly fashion.

Be clear in your introductory statements.

Do not promise things that might not happen.

Direct and arrange the pattern of standing or sitting.

Guide victims with your eyes and voice rather than through physical force.

Use physical force only as a last resort, and only if you are trained and authorized to use it.

Remove the victim from the crisis situation if possible. Be creative in taking control.

Break eye contact between disputants. Separate the victims if necessary.

- Assess the situation.

Evaluate on the spot.

Make the evaluation quick, accurate, and comprehensive.

Do not take a lengthy life history. Focus on the present crisis and the events that precipitated it.

Ask short, direct questions.

Ask questions one at a time.

Allow the victim time to answer.

Do not bombard victims with questions.

Be comfortable with silence.

Avoid interrupting the victim.

Clarify the crisis.

Allow the crisis to be the victim's crisis.

Assess both the actual and the symbolic meaning of the crisis event.

Use the sufferer's body language and nonverbal cues as a source of additional information.

Listen for what is *not* being said.

Recognize that personal attributes can contribute to your effectiveness.

Allow the sufferer to speak freely.

Encourage the sufferer to ventilate feelings.

Establish ground rules in a multiple victim situation.

Return control to the victim as soon as possible.

- Decide how to handle the situation after you have assessed it.

Help victims identify and mobilize their own resources.

Mobilize social resources.

Hold out hope that a solution is possible.

Develop options.

Help parties to the crisis make an agreement.

- Refer as needed.

Have prepared referral information available.

Keep your list of referral sources up to date.

Make appropriate referrals.

- Follow up as agreed.

- Be prepared to repeat steps if necessary. Remain alert, aware, and prepared.
- Use the American Academy of Crisis Interveners Lethality Scale and the Life Change Index Scale if needed.
    Recognize that these are tools to aid in assessment.
    They might be used before, during, or after an intervention. The intervener might decide not to use them.

CHAPTER 3

Communicating Effectively with Those in Crisis

- Determine what the crisis is.
- Identify and address the actual crisis situation.
    Which problem is of most immediate concern?
    Which problem would prove most damaging if not treated immediately?
    Which problem can be most quickly resolved?
    Which problem must be dealt with first before others may be handled?
    What resources for handling problems are available?
    What barriers and obstacles will hinder problem solving?
- Be aware that every communication contains three messages:
    A content message
    A feeling message
    A meaning message
- Be alert to the potential for distortion within a communication.
    What the other person means to say
    What the other person actually says
    What you, as intervener, believe you hear
- Do not assume that you understand.
- Use clarification techniques for understanding:
    Repetition of key words used by victim
    Restatement
    Direct request for clarification
    Use of questions
- Recognize the importance of passive empathy.
- Recognize the importance of active empathy.
- Learn to listen effectively.
- Learn to respond effectively.
- Be alert. *Words do matter.* Choose and use words carefully and purposefully.
- Be aware of *mistaken assumptions* such as:
    "I know exactly how you feel."
    "Listening to and acknowledging feelings implies agreement."
    "If you can't help them, at least don't hurt them." Remember, there is no "non effect."
    "I can relax after the parties are seated."

- Review the list of helpful phrases to get through an impasse.
- Remember that effective intervention can only occur if the intervener and the victim are talking about the *same* crisis.
- Remember that crisis communication can be both loud and silent
  Be alert to nonverbal communication.
  Identify feelings. Refer to Figure 3.
- Refer to the vignettes that appear throughout the book.
- Practice. Practice. Practice.

CHAPTER 4

Team Intervention

- Understand the appropriate use of team intervention:
  For maximizing the safety for all involved
  For efficient information gathering
  For division of responsibility among team members
  For emotional and physical support for team members
- Understand the designation and role of lead teams and lead interveners.
  Clarify the division of responsibility of team members.
  Be familiar with the positioning of team members.
  Be prepared to accept personal responsibility as a team member.
  As a team, apply the procedure for effective Crisis Intervention.

CHAPTER 5

Special Issues for the Intervener

- Reinforce the need for preparation and awareness.
- Recognize the relationship between safety procedures and situational awareness.
- Orient yourself to a mode of safety consciousness.
- Plan for the welfare of crisis victims, interveners, and staff.
- Include receptionists and maintenance people in team safety training. They are often the first people approached.
- Train together and update all as necessary.
- Develop your sensing capabilities.
- Respect inklings, intuitions, and "gut feelings" as red flag alerts.
- Check out something that does not feel/sound/seem right.
- Review the incidents where inklings were ignored.
- Learn to trust your instincts in personal and victim safety.
- Take safety procedures seriously.
  Approach the crisis slowly.
  Don't park in front of the building where the crisis is occurring.
  Approach doors carefully.
  Expect the unexpected.

Listen for clues.
Maintain control.
Visually frisk the people involved.
Remain observant.
Separate disputants if necessary.
Seat the victims.
Sit attentively.
Do not turn your back.
Bring disputants back together.
Maintain eye contact with your partner.
Break eye contact between disputants.
Plan your office with safety in mind.
Intervene with a partner.
Play the "what if" game.
Make contingency plans.
- Be able to identify students at risk for violent behavior.
- Be able to identify adults at risk for violent behavior.
- Be alert to issues of suicide.
  Know what to look for.
  Know what to listen for.
  Some reminders for responding to a suicidal person.
  Act early. Do not leave the sufferer alone.
  Speak of suicide openly.
  Reassure and remain calm.
  Let the sufferer talk.
  Listen carefully and reflect your understanding of the situation.
  Acknowledge his/her hurt.
  Never say, "You don't really want to do that."
  Keep your focus on the present.
  Focus on how to assist the sufferer now.
  Never challenge the victim to "go ahead and do it."
  Help develop options and viable possibilities other than suicide.
  Carefully select anyone you plan to contact. Avoid adding problems.
  Remember that suicide has nothing to do with death.
  Check out the "specificity of the suicidal plan," and the "lethality of the suicidal means."
  Ask the sufferer what he/she plans to do and how.
  You should have a plan in place to cover several possibilities.
- Review and use the vignettes and examples as learning aids.

CHAPTER 6

Intervener Survival   65
- Recognize the signs and symptoms of stress and burnout.
- *Teachable Moment in Crisis Intervention: Intervener's self-care enhances the possibility of a successful intervention.*

- Keep stress within tolerable limits.
- Prevent organizational burnout.
- Use proactive management for reducing stress in the workplace.

CHAPTER 10

Grief, Loss, and Change   98

- Recognize what sufferers might experience during the grief process.
- Remember that the victim's perception is the victim's reality.
- Always clarify the crisis.
- Teach the sufferer to use self-intervention.
- Help the sufferer cope with separation or loss.
- *Teachable Moment: Slowly, slowly one heals. Often the reminder to take baby steps is the most important message that the victim remembers.*
- Recognize the recurring reactions of sufferers of tragic events.
- Feelings associated with dying.
- Follow the guidelines for intervening with a dying person who is in crisis.
- An intervener must address his/her own feelings concerning death/ dying before attempting to manage the sufferer's grief.
- Recognize the recurring reactions of sufferers of tragic events.
- Read and use the vignettes and examples to strengthen your skills.

- Know the laws that govern what you do.
- Treat victims as human beings rather than as cases.
- Intervene within the limits of your background, training, and experience.
- If you begin an intervention, stay with it unless you are relieved by
- someone with greater skill.
- If possible, obtain consent before intervening.
- Maintain confidentiality of all information you obtain.
- Document all your actions in an intervention.
- Maintain your professional competency.
- Respect the victim's right to privacy.
- Think before you act.

- Prepare to respond to a disaster.
- Take care of yourself.
- Apply Crisis Intervention procedure.
- Respond to victims' need for information.
- Review effective disaster communications skills.
- Use translators effectively.

Preface

From Stepchild to Discipline:

Are We There Yet?

A third edition of a book would suggest that there continues to be an audience for whom the subject matter has appeal and/or curiosity. Crisis and the management of crises have become front and center in our daily lives. Increasingly, the news media, the blogs, the discussions at the dinner table, and the conversations around the office water cooler focus on the crisis de jour. There is a ripple effect of anxiety, concern, sadness, and grief that we share to a greater or lesser degree. We can hear the voices of the sufferers, and today's technology allows us to see their hurt up close regardless of the geographical distance that separates us. At any given time 24/7, an individual intervener, a team of interveners, or multiple teams are responding and they are providing emotional first aid in crisis situations.

Programs designed to deal with human crises have existed for many years. As a result of unusually high stress brought on by certain events that may occur without warning and in a sudden fashion, a person may experience an inability to cope with life in the way he or she would under more normal conditions. Rape, natural disasters, domestic disputes, man-made disasters and the like can each produce sufficient stress to create a crisis. Interested groups, lay persons, helping professionals, and crisis-oriented agencies have sprung up to offer assistance in such situations.

Early studies of the victims of man-made disasters and families affected by wartime deaths set the stage for what has been emerging as the modern discipline of Crisis Intervention, or Crisis Management. As techniques developed, they were applied to many diverse fields, including law enforcement, penology, social service, business, religion, and nursing. Many definitions of Crisis Intervention appeared and, as the term gained professional acceptance, books and papers were written under this popular heading, covering topics from psychotherapeutic techniques to short-term therapy. Yet Crisis Intervention was regarded as the stepchild to all other helping disciplines, such as sociology, psychology, and psychiatry, while having little or no fixed and recognized place of its own. Few academic institutions addressed this particular area separately, and it was seen as part of some larger psychotherapeutic or counseling concern. It was thought that good counselors also made good crisis interveners; those who could handle day-to-day counseling sessions were assumed to be quite capable of intervening in emergencies and severe stress-related incidents.

It became increasingly clear that psychotherapeutic experience does not in itself supply Crisis Intervention expertise. In order to fully understand crises and intervention into such situations, specific definitions, procedures, and training are essential. In short, Crisis Management must be recognized as a professional discipline with a tradition, a definite place in today's professional and paraprofessional community, and a future within the overall health care system. It must have its own professionals, organizations, training academies, certifications, journals, and recognition to allow its development as a significant and viable scientific entity.

A complete history of the movement is an important subject for another book. The Greenstone & Leviton book *Hotline: Crisis Intervention Directory*, 1981 provides a comprehensive background. However, the authors believe it is important to mention briefly the genesis of our decision to spend 40-plus years doing the groundwork necessary to help establish Crisis Intervention as a discipline.

In 1969, The Southern Indiana Chapter of the National Conference of Christians and Jews began a project in Louisville, Kentucky, designed to provide training in community relations and Crisis Intervention. As it developed, the project gave professionals, paraprofessionals, and nonprofessionals training and experience in techniques of Crisis Management that could prevent serious emotional upsets from becoming disastrous to the people involved. Three years later, an offshoot of this initial program was established to show that Crisis Intervention procedures and principles could be applied to any crisis situation. For example, the methods used by police officers could be employed by crisis center counselors. The major proponents of this interdisciplinary approach were Dr. Edward S. Rosenbluh and Dr. James L. Greenstone, who began piecing it together in 1963 while at the University of Oklahoma; Lieutenant James E. Oney of the Louisville Division of Police; and Dr. Kent A. Rensin, a former police officer and high school administrator.

From these beginnings, the National Institute for Training in Crisis Intervention emerged. There, on a regularly scheduled basis students of Crisis Management, regardless of professional credentials, could receive specific and expert training. The National Institute laid the groundwork in 1976 for the formation of the American Academy of Crisis Interveners, which served as the first national attempt to unify and organize the field of Crisis Intervention. Crisis workers in all settings could now identify with their own organization rather than being subsumed as part of another group. The Southwestern Academy of Crisis Interveners formed in 1978 with Dr. Sharon C. Leviton as its executive director. The Southeastern Academy was formed shortly afterward by Dr. W. Rodney Fowler, Former Professor and Head of Graduate Programs in Counseling at the University of Tennessee at Chattanooga. Subsequently, the National Training Conference for Crisis Intervention developed and offered graduated levels of training in Crisis Intervention. Following the introduction of basic, intermediate, and advanced levels of Crisis Management training, a certification program was established to allow any crisis worker who qualified to be certified within his/her own discipline. In 1980, The American Board of Examiners in Crisis Intervention (ABECI) was established for that purpose. All training adhered to the interdisciplinary concept that permits not only the needed social interaction among agencies but also the sharing of their skills to the mutual benefit of all.

The alliance in 2002 of The American College of Forensic Examiners International (ACEFI) and the American Board of Examiners in Crisis Intervention (ABECI) was welcomed by those of us who have labored for years to advance Crisis Intervention as a discipline of its own.

How do we know if we are there yet? Certification is certainly one marker of accomplishment and success. The applicant's ability to have passed the written, the oral, and the practical portions of the Certification exam along with fulfilling the requirement to submit an original paper suitable for publication is a significant accomplishment. However, that should not be viewed as an education completed. If Crisis Intervention is to be considered a viable and relevant discipline, the practitioners must commit to ongoing study; to ongoing participation in team training; to making contributions to the body of knowledge through writing/teaching/research; and to be held to an established set of standards of practice. The intervener must take personal responsibility for being prepared mentally, physically, and emotionally. Being aware and being prepared speaks to how seriously an intervener takes his/her profession.

Elements of Crisis Intervention is intended for the following groups of people:

Crisis workers
Hot-line workers
Parents
Teachers
Counselors and psychotherapists
Support group members and leaders
Outreach groups
Managers and supervisors
Agency directors
Disaster workers
First responders
Military personnel
Police officers
Nurses
Grief counselors
Firefighters
Probation and parole officers

Peer counselors
Emergency medical service personnel
Social workers
School-based crisis management teams
School violence counselors
School crisis response team members
Hostage negotiators
Clergy
Flight attendants
Judiciary
Government agency personnel
Mediators
Secondary victims
Receptionists

We have reduced the practice of Crisis Intervention to its basic elements so these elements can be applied as broadly as possible, and we present them in a format that is useful both for the experienced professional and for the novice. We know of no other text that approaches the subject so directly. We have spent much time in our careers eliminating confusion about procedures and about the relationship between Crisis Intervention and other behavioral sciences. This book reinforces the theoretical framework that postulates Crisis Intervention as a viable discipline in itself.

Because this is a practical guide, most theory has been purposely omitted. We suggest that *Elements of Crisis Intervention* be used as a supplement in classes in psychology, counseling, psychotherapy, crisis intervention, crisis counseling, health services, emergency medicine, police science, negotiations, school-based crisis management plans, and in other related practical and applied courses at all levels. It is also appropriate for training courses in Crisis Intervention and Crisis Counseling. The experienced intervener can use the book independently, in the classroom, in the office, and in the field.

How to Use This Book

This book is designed to aid in practical, day-to-day, on-the-scene Crisis Intervention. In addition to listing the areas covered in the chapters, the table of contents is a step-by-step guide to the intervention process and should be used by interveners to guide an intervention in an orderly fashion. For the experienced crisis intervener, the table of contents is a helpful reminder of the steps that should be taken during an intervention. Novices may need to read the entire book carefully before they can use the table of contents effectively, and they should understand that that the full value of this book depends on their gaining theoretical depth and practical training.

Interveners can also look up material according to the activity they want to perform or by the intervener's role (for example, police officer or therapist). These listings are printed on the inside front and back covers of the book.

The Elements of Crisis Intervention

A crisis occurs when unusual stress temporarily renders an individual unable to direct life effectively. As the stress mounts and the usual coping mechanisms provide neither relief nor remedy, the person often experiences extreme feelings of fear, anger, grief, hostility, hopelessness, helplessness, and alienation from self, family, and society. Crisis can be a reaction to a single event or to several events occurring simultaneously or serially.

Ordinary upsets can be handled with day-to-day skills. Crises happen suddenly and unexpectedly and seem arbitrary. Inexplicable events raise stress to a critical level. Crisis Intervention is a timely and skillful intrusion into a personal crisis to defuse a potentially disastrous situation before physical or emotional destruction occurs. The intervener attempts to return the sufferer to a level of pre-crisis functioning at a time when his/her life lacks structure. Rosenbluh (1975) calls this "emotional first aid." Just as people bleed physically, they can also bleed—and bleed to death—emotionally. Crisis Intervention is not therapy; it is the skilled attempt to stop the emotional bleeding in a way that will allow the individual to continue life effectively. The intervener makes quick, accurate, critical decisions about the victim and mobilizes needed resources. Successful Crisis Intervention achieves problem management, not problem resolution. The intervener who has helped the victim of a crisis regain pre-crisis stability has met the goal of Crisis Intervention. Although an individual may require support after a crisis that can include psychotherapy or counseling, effective Crisis Intervention can significantly reduce the need for intensive treatment.

To a great extent, we apply the theory that "A crisis is a crisis is a crisis" (Leviton, 1982, p. 10). Although we can certainly argue that a particular incident requires a specific response, that incident-specific response is always grounded in the basic Crisis Intervention theory and procedures that are the subject of this book. As Rosenbluh puts it, "If we are to be helpful, we must remain effective" (1975), and the keys to effectiveness are having a clear understanding of the elements of Crisis Intervention and the ability to apply them practically. A return to the basics is nearly always beneficial, and is continually instructive, to all who work in the discipline of Crisis Intervention.

New to This Edition

Elements of Crisis Intervention has been updated to include new topics, expand the scope of several areas discussed in the prior editions, and reinforce the key elements that define effective Crisis Management. The new material includes the following:

1. Disaster response—The emphasis is on preparation, awareness, personal readiness, intervention procedures, safety issues, intervener survival issues, and disaster crisis

communications. Multiple vignettes and verbal exchanges are included. Lists of "dos" and "don'ts"; practical, on the scene type of information is provided; and the pre- and post-deployment physical, emotional, and psychological needs of the intervener are addressed.

2. Safety—The emphasis in this edition is on the relationship between safety procedures and personal and situational awareness. The authors call special attention to the importance of "inklings," or red flags, and one's intuition as warning signals of possible danger. The accompanying vignettes illustrate how people often know that something is not right or fear that a particular person or a place is wrong for them. They dismiss the inkling as silly or inappropriate without further examination. Unfortunately, this occurs in dating and mating where the stakes are high.

3. Suicide—What to look for and how to respond to a suicidal person.

4. Use of translators in Crisis Intervention—The qualifications, selection process, and limits of the role are provided.

5. Grief: An expanded discussion of change, loss, and grief as the underpinning of crisis situations.

6. "Teachable Moments," "mistaken assumptions," and other "take notice" signals—These appear in various places in the book and are brief but important messages.

7. Words matter—Emphasis is placed on how the careful choice of words matter in crisis communications. Examples of what works and what does not work are presented. Sometimes an intervener feels stuck. The authors present a list of words and phrases to help move you through the impasse.

The themes of awareness, preparation, durability, and resilience appear throughout the book. There is no doubt that the "new normal" of life post 9/11 has fostered the urgency for interveners to be ready and fit to respond.

James L. Greenstone
Sharon C. Leviton

Approach to Crisis Intervention

What Is a Crisis?

A crisis occurs when unusual stress temporarily renders an individual unable to direct life effectively. As the stress mounts and the usual coping mechanisms provide neither relief nor remedy, the person often experiences extreme feelings of grief, hostility, helplessness, hopelessness, and alienation from self, family, and society. Stress can be a reaction to a single event or to several events occurring simultaneously or serially.

Over their lifetime, people develop assumptions and points of view that color and determine their behavior. They act daily in accordance with these concepts and deeply held beliefs. This may be why something that seems crisis producing to one person may be quite ordinary to another. The need to identify the victim's perception of the crisis event is a key element in effective Crisis Intervention. The way the crisis victim currently perceives the world is the victim's reality.

Ordinary upsets can be handled with day-to-day skills. Crises happen suddenly and unexpectedly and seem arbitrary. Inexplicable events raise stress to a critical level. Crisis Intervention is a timely and skillful intrusion into a personal crisis to diffuse a potentially disastrous situation before physical or emotional destruction occurs. The intervener attempts to return the sufferer to a level of pre-crisis functioning at a time when his or her life lacks structure. Rosenbluh (1975) calls this "emotional first aid." Just as people bleed physically, they can also bleed—and bleed to death—emotionally. Crisis Intervention is not therapy. It is the skilled attempt to stop the emotional bleeding in a way that will allow the individual to continue life effectively. The intervener makes quick, accurate, critical decisions about the victim and mobilizes needed resources. Crisis Intervention is to emergency-room medicine what a medical practice is to a psychotherapy practice. Psychotherapy and Crisis Intervention must never be confused. To do so could deny what victims need at a critical time in their lives. To be sure, every therapist will benefit from developing Crisis Intervention skills, but to assume that Crisis Intervention and counseling are the same is courting disaster (see Corsini, 1981). Successful Crisis Intervention achieves problem management, not problem resolution. The intervener who has helped the victim of a crisis regain pre-crisis stability has met the goals of Crisis Intervention. Although a person may require support after a crisis that can include psychotherapy or counseling, effective Crisis Intervention can significantly reduce the need for intensive treatment.

The crisis cube is a three-dimensional representation of crisis development (see Figure 1.1). The crisis cube illustrates how, before a crisis, the normal level of functioning can be interrupted by the occurrence of unusual stress caused by single, multiple, or serial factors. When this happens, a person attempts to solve problems and handle the tension in usual ways. As the attempts fail and the tension mounts, a downward spiral of ineffective behavior, referred to as maladaptive behavior, occurs. The intervener's job is to interrupt the downward spiral as skillfully and as quickly as possible and, in doing so, return the sufferer to pre-crisis level of functioning. As the timeline on the crisis cube indicates, every moment is crucial to the intervener. The longer the line of maladaptive behavior goes unchallenged and uninterrupted, the greater is the possibility of increased personality disintegration and increased need for psychological treatment or therapy after the crisis is over. The intervener's skill and the timeliness of the intervention can determine the possibility of the victim's later functioning and growth.

The following are indicators of a person who may be prone to crisis. We also present a list of precipitating factors. Finally, signs and symptoms of a person in crisis are presented as a guide to recognition of and need for intervention. These events must be understood from the sufferers' perspectives of what the crisis is for them.

INDICATORS THAT CAN CHARACTERIZE A CRISIS-PRONE PERSON

- Alienation from lasting and meaningful personal relationships
- Inability to use life support systems such as family, friends, and social groups
- Difficulty in learning from experience; the individual continues to make the same mistakes

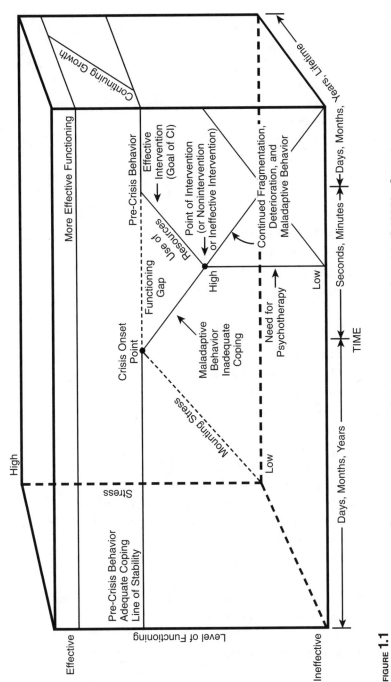

FIGURE 1.1

The Crisis Cube. From *Handbook of Crisis Interveners* by Greenstone and Leviton. Copyright © 1982 by Greenstone. Reprinted with permission of Kendall/Hunt Publishing Co.

3

- A history of previously experienced crises that have not been effectively resolved
- A history of mental disorder or severe emotional imbalance
- Feelings of low self-esteem
- Neglectful of personal needs, personal safety, and responsibility for self-direction
- Unwillingness to understand the relationship between actions and consequences
- Provocative, impulsive behavior resulting from unresolved inner conflict
- A history of poor marital relationships
- Excessive use of drugs, including alcohol abuse
- Marginal income
- Lack of regular, fulfilling work
- Unusual or frequent physical injuries
- Frequent changes in residence
- Frequent encounters with the law

EVENTS THAT CAN PRECIPITATE A CRISIS

- An accident in the home
- An automobile or airplane accident, with or without injury
- Being arrested; appearing in court
- Changes in job situation and income involving either promotion or demotion
- Military deployments
- Death of a significant person in one's life
- Divorce or separation
- A delinquency episode either in childhood or adulthood (in childhood, skipping school or running away from home; in adulthood, failure to pay debts)
- Entry into school
- Abortion or out-of-wedlock pregnancy
- Physical illness and the impact on the patient and the family
- Acute episodes of mental disorder
- Retirement
- Natural disasters or man-made disasters or pandemics
- Sexual difficulties
- Major change in living conditions

- Gaining a new family member (for example, through birth, adoption, or parents or adult children moving in)
- Dealing with a blended family
- Foreclosure on a mortgage or loan
- Actual or impending loss of something significant in one's life
- Episodes of abuse

Although a particular stressful situation might not induce crisis, a combination of several such stressful events could push the individual to the crisis point.

RECOGNIZING A PERSON IN CRISIS

1. Recognition depends on
   a. The intervener's awareness of what the victim is communicating verbally and nonverbally
   b. The intervener's sensing capabilities
2. Different people indicate crisis in different ways:
   a. Crying out, exploding, verbalizing
   b. Withdrawal, depression, or both
3. If possible, the intervener should obtain information from family and friends about the victim's pre-crisis behavior and note disruptions in previous behavior and modes of ineffective functioning.
4. Profile of a person in crisis:
   a. Bewilderment: "I never felt this way before."
   b. Danger: "I am so nervous and scared."
   c. Confusion: "I can't think clearly."
   d. Impasse: "I feel stuck; nothing I do helps."
   e. Desperation: "I've got to do something."
   f. Apathy: "Nothing can help me."
   g. Helplessness: "I can't take care of myself."
   h. Urgency: "I need help now!!!"
   i. Discomfort: "I feel miserable, restless, and unsettled."
   j. Numbness: "I don't feel anything . . . anything. It's all surreal."

At this point, the victim is not totally in control of his or her life and feels the panic resulting from this realization. Victims may flail about emotionally, verbally, or even physically as they experience this lack of control.

COMMON SIGNS AND SYMPTOMS OF PSYCHOLOGICAL REACTIONS
TO CRISIS

Emotional

Anticipatory anxiety
Generalized anxiety
Shock
Denial
Insecurity
Fatigue
Uncertainty
Fear
Helplessness
Depression
Panic

Despair
Survivor guilt
Feeling out of control
Grief
Outrage
Numbness
Frustration
Inadequacy
Feeling overwhelmed
Anger
Irritability

Cognitive

Confusion
Poor attention span
Poor concentration
Flashbacks

Loss of trust
Difficulties in decision making
Nightmares

Behavioral

Withdrawal
Sleep disturbances
Angry outbursts
Change in activity
Change in appetite
Increased fatigue
Excessive use of sick leave
Alcohol or drug abuse
Difficulty functioning at normal
    ability level
Antisocial acts
Frequent visits to physician for
    nonspecific complaints

Anger at God
Loss of desire to attend
    religious services
Regression
Crying
Change in communications
Preoccupation with the crisis to
    the exclusion of other areas
    of life
Diminished job performance
Unresponsiveness
Hysterical reactions
Irritability

Procedures for Effective Crisis Intervention

The Need for an Established Procedure

Crisis interveners learn early in their careers that having an established procedure to follow is vital to their effectiveness. An intervention is a logical and orderly process. Step-by-step the intervener/responder assists the sufferer in moving from a state of disequilibrium to at least his or her pre-crisis level of functioning.

The time to develop a procedure is before attempting to intervene. Every action and every interaction must be thoughtful, measured, and purposeful. This is not a time to say "I'll try this out and see what happens." Such a haphazard approach would court disaster for the victim and intervener.

Crisis situations can and do occur at inconvenient and odd times of the day, night, weekend, or holidays. When the phone rings in the middle of the night and the voice on the other end says "I'm going to kill myself," the prepared intervener will automatically access his or her proven plan of response. Having the ability to mentally run through a checklist provides the comfort of knowing that all the steps were covered.

The authors have used the following Crisis Intervention model for the past 40 years. While the individual crises may differ and the individual interveners will use their personal skill sets to respond, the model and principles presented here can be applied to nearly all crisis situations.

Crisis Intervention consists of six major components (see Figure 2.1):

I. IMMEDIACY	IV. DISPOSITION
II. CONTROL	V. REFERRAL
III. ASSESSMENT	VI. FOLLOW-UP

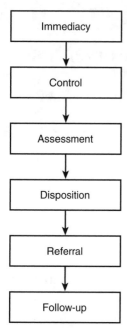

FIGURE 2.1
Crisis Intervention procedure

In the authors' experience, to eliminate, bypass, or rearrange the order of the six steps is counterproductive. However, it may become necessary during some interventions to repeat steps. Examples: if the sufferer became highly agitated after the intervention had been moving smoothly; or the real crisis was not revealed or identified during the assessment; or it became obvious that the sufferer had shut down. At some point in their career, interveners will deal with this. Being aware and being prepared are key elements in effective response to the unexpected.

The following outlines describe effective Crisis Intervention procedures.

I. Act immediately to stop the emotional bleeding.

Intervention begins at the moment the intervener/responder encounters the person in crisis. The intervener must immediately attempt to

- Relieve anxiety
- Prevent further disorientation
- Ensure that sufferers do not harm themselves or cause harm to others

II. *Take control.*

a. Be clear about what and whom you are attempting to control.

The purpose of assuming control is not to conquer or overwhelm the victim. Rather, it is to help reorder the chaos that exists in the sufferer's world at the moment of crisis. The intervener/responder provides the needed structure until the victim can regain control.

b. Enter the crisis scene cautiously.

Approach any crisis situation slowly and carefully. Caution at this point can prevent unnecessary grief. Take a moment to mentally compute what you

- Hear
- See
- Smell
- Feel
- Sense
- Touch

c. Appear stable, supportive, and able to establish structure.

Use your personal presence. Your strength, control, and calm in the crisis situation may exert the control the victim needs.

d. Be clear in your introductory statements. The opening questions, directions, and other information you give the victim will often assist in gaining and in maintaining control.

INTERVENER: *Hello, I'm Sharon Leviton from the Crisis Center. Are you Mrs. Jones?*
MRS. JONES: *Yes. I don't know what you or anybody else can do. I just know . . . I can't stand it anymore.*
INTERVENER: *I'd like to listen to what's bothering you. May I come in?*

e. Do not promise things that might not happen. For example, don't say, "I can fix it. Everything will be all right." It might not be!
f. Direct and arrange the pattern of standing and sitting to gain the victim's attention.
g. Guide the sufferer with your eyes and voice rather than through physical force.

   h. Use physical force only as a last resort, and only if you are trained and authorized to use it.

   i. Remove the victim from the crisis situation if possible. Otherwise, remove the crisis from the victim.

   j. Be creative in taking control.

   k. Break eye contact between disputants.

   l. Separate the victims if necessary.

Specific ways of gaining control in a crisis situation vary, depending on the skills and abilities of the intervener. The task allows wide latitude for creativity. Possible ways of taking control include the following:

- Creating a loud noise to gain attention.
- Speaking in a quieter tone than the victim is.
- Breaking eye contact between two disputants to reduce tension.
- Making an odd request: "May I see that book over there?"

Victims will respond to structure and to those who represent it if they sense it is genuine and not just a technique.

III. Assess the situation.

- What is troubling the victim now?
- Why did the person go into crisis at this particular time? What recently happened?
- Which problem among those that might be present is of immediate concern?
- Which problem must be dealt with before other problems can be handled?
- Which problem among those presented can be immediately managed?
- What variables will hinder the problem-management process?
- How can the intervener implement the most effective help in the least time?

To accomplish an effective assessment, do the following:

   a. Evaluate on the spot. Don't wait.

   b. Make the evaluation quick, accurate, and comprehensive enough to give a total picture.

   c. Do not take a lengthy life history. Focus the assessment on the present crisis and the events that occurred within the last 48 hours. What were the precipitating events?

INTERVENER: *Tell me what happened in the last few days.*
MARY: *I lost my job today.*
INTERVENER: *Your job was important to you.*
MARY: *Yes. I have to have it because my husband walked out on me yesterday.*
INTERVENER: *You seem very frightened.*
MARY: *I'm scared to death. My husband left me. I've got three little babies. My mom is dying of cancer, and I don't have a job. We're three months behind in the rent. I've got nowhere to turn. There's no way I'm going to make it. I've got nowhere to go, so I may as well end it. My kids would be better off . . .*

d. Ask short, direct questions.

INTERVENER: *How are you feeling, John?*
JOHN: *I feel lost and strange.*
INTERVENER: *What do you mean by "strange"?*
JOHN: *I can't explain it.*
INTERVENER: *Can you put another feeling with strange?*
JOHN: *Hopeless. I can't find any way to cope with Judy's death.*

e. Ask questions one at a time.
f. Allow the victim enough time to answer your questions.

INTERVENER: *Did you ever feel this way before?*
(Pause)
JOHN: *I can't think too clearly. That's what is so scary to me.*
INTERVENER: *Take your time, John. We're in no rush.*

g. Do not increase victims' confusion by bombarding them with many questions at once.
h. Learn to accept discomfort with silence. Recognize the usefulness of silence in the intervention process.
i. Interrupt the victim judiciously. You can use periodic interruptions to clarify, to check the accuracy and your understanding of the victim's statements, and simply to remind the victim of your interest in the problem. Interrupt no more often than absolutely necessary.
j. Clarify the crisis. To be effective you must know what the crisis is.

INTERVENER: *Your fear of your dad finding out about your pregnancy seems to be causing your feelings of terror.*

ANN: *That's most of it. I disappointed and embarrassed him. He'll abandon me. He'll slap my mom around and blame her. I ruined it for everybody! I've got to run away.*

k. Allow the crisis to be the victim's crisis. Avoid judgments, preachments, and putdowns. Don't belittle the victim or the crisis; crisis is always in the eye of the beholder. The way the victim currently perceives the world is the victim's reality. For example, don't say, "You're silly to be so worried. He wasn't worth it anyway. I know you'll find someone else next week."

l. Assess both the actual and the symbolic meaning of the crisis event. Remember that perception triggers crisis much more often than do facts.

m. Use the sufferer's body language and nonverbal behavior as a source of information. If you observe that the words and behavior do not match, question the discrepancy.

n. Listen for what is not being said. Attend to what the victim says and does. Be aware of what the victim has not done and what would normally be expected under current circumstances.

o. Recognize that your personal attributes contribute to your overall effectiveness.
   • Remain reassuring and calm.
   • Remain empathic and attentive.
   • Remain supportive.
   • Be willing to reach out to the sufferer, both physically and emotionally, as needed.
   • Maintain a caring attitude that conveys a willingness to listen.

p. Allow the victim to speak freely and to ventilate feelings.

q. Help the victim to see the crisis as temporary rather than chronic.

r. In a multiple-victim situation (such as a family dispute), allow each person to speak without interruption by the other people involved. Establish ground rules immediately, and insist they be followed.

INTERVENER: *Mr. Jones, will you agree to listen while your wife talks to us?*

MR. JONES: *But she never shuts up.*

INTERVENER: *I will ensure that each of you has enough time to say what you need to. I'm very interested in hearing both of you.*

MR. JONES: *OK, I'll agree to that. But she better be careful. You have to watch her.*

INTERVENER: *Mrs. Jones, will you agree to listen while Mr. Jones talks?*

MRS. JONES: *Oh, yes. You can count on me.*

s. Return control to the victim as soon as possible.

IV. Decide how to handle the situation after you have assessed it.

Heightened stress closes down options and generally produces "tunnel vision" in the victim. When effective intervention occurs, the victim becomes more receptive to

- Exploring options
- Thinking creatively
- Solving problems

a. Help the victim identify and mobilize personal resources.

INTERVENER: *Mrs. Smith, what is one way that you might manage that trapped feeling when John is out of town?*

MRS. SMITH: *I can call the lady next door and trade babysitting with her.*

INTERVENER: *Would you feel comfortable with that?*

MRS. SMITH: *She's very caring and responsible, and it could be good for the kids and for me. I wouldn't get so angry and upset with the kids. I can't believe what I almost did.*

INTERVENER: *Do you have any other ideas?*

MRS. SMITH: *John and I need some professional help about a few things. Could you help me find a family counselor? I'm ready to get on with this.*

INTERVENER: *Yes, I can.*

b. Mobilize social resources.
c. Hold out hope that solutions are possible.
d. Develop options.
e. Help the parties to the crisis make an agreement.

Almost any agreement answers the following questions:

- Who?
- What?

- Where?
- When?
- Why?
- What if?
- How much?

MR. JONES: *I'll babysit on Tuesday evenings so Mary can take care of her dad.*
INTERVENER: *What time on Tuesday?*
MR. JONES: *I can get home by 5:00 P.M. Remember, I can't keep this up after January.*
INTERVENER: *So, after January, Mary will have to make other plans about the visitation.*
MRS. JONES: *I understand. The pressure should be over by then.*
INTERVENER: *What if you can't babysit on Tuesday at that time?*
MR. JONES: *I'll be responsible for making other arrangements.*

V. *Refer as needed. Follow up if possible or as agreed.*

a. Investigate possible referral sources by checking local telephone directories and manuals that list specialized services.
b. Check with professionals such as doctors, lawyers, and clergy in the community. Determine if they take referrals from crisis situations; not all do. Ask if they would be on call to assist if needed.
c. Contact local hospital emergency care units and get to know the staff. Find out about requirements for admission and treatment.
d. Visit agencies in the community that provide assistance to crisis victims. Find out if they are willing and equipped to accept referrals and if they will
   (1) give a crisis-victim referral high priority in scheduling,
   (2) understand the need for proper crisis referrals, and
   (3) give feedback when an intervener tries to follow up with someone who has been referred.
e. Determine the hours of operation of each potential referral agency. Are the agencies staffed by people or answering machines?
f. Make a list of acceptable referral sources.
g. Be sure the phone numbers, addresses, and names of contact persons are current.

  h. Determine what state and national referral agencies or hot lines crisis victims can access.

  i. Update your referral list regularly. Add reliable agencies once you have checked them. Eliminate unreliable agencies as your experience with each dictates. Delete agencies that no longer provide the needed crisis services.

  j. Determine the required fees for services and acceptable methods of payment.

  k. Determine which agencies will accept referrals of crisis victims with limited financial resources.

  l. Know the availability of transportation to and from the referral source. Sometimes the lack of this information will cause the referral process to break down even though other aspects of the intervention have been properly conducted.

  m. Find out if the offices of the referral source have made provisions for persons with physical disabilities.

  n. Have your list of referral sources available for use during an intervention.

  o. When you are making a referral, do the following:

    (1) Print the information about the referral source on a card or piece of paper for the victim.

    (2) Carefully review the information with the victim.

    (3) In a telephone intervention, give the referral information slowly, clearly, and concisely. Ask the victim to repeat the information you have given and to write down the information if possible.

    (4) If you feel it might be helpful, help the victim make contact with the referral agency. For example, place the call to the agency from your office.

    (5) Double-check the accuracy of the referral information you provide to the victim or the family.

    (6) Ask the victim if the information is clear and understandable.

    (7) Ask victims if they know of any circumstance that would prevent their making contact with the referral agency or keeping an appointment with the agency.

    (8) If problems are identified, attempt to deal with them on the spot.

VI. *Follow up with victims to ensure that they made contact with the referral agency.*

    a. If the victim has not made contact with the referral agency within a reasonable amount of time, try to find out why.

    b. If necessary, attempt to help victims deal with their reasons for not contacting the referral agency.

    c. Re-refer victims as appropriate.

Two Useful Tools to Aid in Assessment

Tables 2.1 and 2.2 can help interveners with their assessments. We have found these useful tools in recognizing what is going on with an individual because they aid in our sensitivity to that person's situation.

The scales might be used before, during, or after an intervention. The intervener might decide not to use them.

The following are explanations for each category on the American Academy of Crisis Interveners Lethality Scale (Table 2.1) and the Life Change Index Scale (Table 2.2):

Age: Self-explanatory
Stress: At what level is the victim experiencing stress?
Resources: Personal, family, and social support available
Marital status: Self-explanatory
Psychological functioning: Person's functioning before this event
Symptoms: Self-explanatory
Communications: General level of interpersonal interaction
Physical condition: Self-explanatory
Suicide by close family member: History of suicide in immediate family
Depressed/agitated: Self-explanatory
Prior suicidal behavior: History of attempts
Reaction by significant others: Self-explanatory
Financial stress: Self-explanatory
Suicidal plan: Current plan and specificity
Occupation: Self-explanatory
Residence: Self-explanatory
Living arrangements: Self-explanatory

TABLE 2.1	**AMERICAN ACADEMY OF CRISIS INTERVENERS LETHALITY SCALE**

Date _____ **Name** _____

Criteria:
Minimal risk	(0–15)	_____
Low risk	(16–30)	_____
Medium risk	(31–46)	_____
High risk	(47–60)	_____

Circle response in appropriate row and column and place score from top column in extreme right column. Sum all scores and match total with criteria.

		0	1	2	3	4	Score
Age	Male	0–12		13–44	45–64	65+	
	Female	0–12	13–44	45+			
Stress		Low		Medium		High	
Resources		Good	Fair		Poor		
Marital Status		Married with children	Married without children		Widowed, Single	Divorced	
Psychological Functioning		Stable			Unstable		
Symptoms (alcoholism, drug addiction, homosexuality)		Absent			Present		
Communications		Open			Blocked		
Physical Condition		Good	Fair			Poor	
Suicide by Close Family Member		No		Yes			
Depressed/ Agitated		No				Yes	
Prior Suicidal Behavior		No		Yes			
Reaction by Significant Others		Helpful			Not helpful		
Financial Stress		Absent		Present			
Suicidal Plan		None	Few details	Means Selected		Highly Specific Plan	
Occupation		Non-helping profession, Other Occupation	M.D., Dentist, Attorney, Helping profession	Psychiatrist, Police officer, Unemployed			

(continued)

TABLE 2.1	AMERICAN ACADEMY OF CRISIS INTERVENERS LETHALITY SCALE (CONTINUED)					
	0	1	2	3	4	Score
Residence	Rural	Suburban	Urban			
Living Arrangements	With others				Alone	
Time of Year		Spring				
Day of Week		Sunday, Wednesday	Monday			
Serious Arguments with Spouse	No	Yes				
Loss of Significant Other (Recently)		Focus of disappointment				

Intervener _____   Total _____

Reprinted with permission of A.A.C.I.

Time of year: Current time of year

Day of week: Day of week crisis is occurring

Serious arguments with spouse: Self-explanatory

Significant other: Someone close to the victim who has disappointed or been lost to the victim through death, desertion, or divorce

Interpreting Your Score

Dr. Thomas Holmes and his colleagues have clearly shown the relationship between recent life changes and future illness. The following are score categories and the associated probability of illness during the next two years for a person with that score:

0–150	No significant problem
150–199	Mild Life Crisis Level with a 35% chance of illness
200–299	Moderate Life Crisis Level with a 50% chance of illness
300 or over	Major Life Crisis Level with an 80% chance of illness

More than your life change unit (LCU) total score is related to your likelihood of illness. How you respond to changes and the amount of

TABLE 2.2	LIFE CHANGE INDEX SCALE

Look over the events listed in the Life Change Index Scale. Place a check (÷) in the space next to a given event if it has happened to you within the last twelve months.

1.	Death of a spouse	1.	_____	100
2.	Divorce	2.	_____	73
3.	Marital separation from mate	3.	_____	65
4.	Detention in jail or other institution	4.	_____	63
5.	Death of a close family member	5.	_____	63
6.	Major personal injury or illness	6.	_____	53
7.	Marriage	7.	_____	50
8.	Being fired at work	8.	_____	47
9.	Marital reconciliation	9.	_____	45
10.	Retirement from work	10.	_____	45
11.	Major change in the health or behavior of a family member	11.	_____	44
12.	Pregnancy	12.	_____	40
13.	Sexual difficulties	13.	_____	39
14.	Gaining a new family member (e.g., through birth, adoption, oldster moving in, etc.)	14.	_____	39
15.	Major business readjustment (e.g., merger, reorganization, bankruptcy, etc.)	15.	_____	38
16.	Major change in financial state (e.g., either a lot worse off or a lot better off than usual)	16.	_____	37
17.	Death of a close friend	17.	_____	36
18.	Changing to a different line of work	18.	_____	36
19.	Major change in the number of arguments with spouse (e.g., either a lot more or a lot less than usual regarding child-rearing, personal habits, etc.)	19.	_____	35
20.	Taking on a mortgage greater than $10,000 (e.g., purchasing a home, business, etc.)	20.	_____	31
21.	Foreclosure on a mortgage or loan	21.	_____	30
22.	Major change in responsibilities at work (e.g., promotion, demotion, lateral transfer)	22.	_____	29
23.	Son or daughter leaving home (e.g., marriage, attending college, etc.)	23.	_____	29
24.	In-law troubles	24.	_____	29
25.	Outstanding personal achievement	25.	_____	28
26.	Spouse beginning or ceasing work outside the home	26.	_____	26
27.	Beginning or ceasing formal schooling	27.	_____	26
28.	Major change in living conditions (e.g., building a new home, remodeling, deterioration of home or neighborhood)	28.	_____	25
29.	Revision of personal habits (dress, manners, associations, etc.)	29.	_____	24
30.	Troubles with the boss	30.	_____	23
31.	Major change in working hours or conditions	31.	_____	20
32.	Change in residence	32.	_____	20
33.	Change to a new school	33.	_____	20
34.	Major change in usual type and/or amount of recreation	34.	_____	19
35.	Major change in church activities (e.g., a lot more or less than usual)	35.	_____	19

(continued)

	TABLE
	2.2

LIFE CHANGE INDEX SCALE (CONTINUED)

36.	Major change in social activities (e.g., clubs, dancing, movies, visiting, etc.)	36. _____	18
37.	Taking on a mortgage or loan less than $10,000 (e.g., purchasing a car, TV, freezer, etc.)	37. _____	17
38.	Major change in sleeping habits (a lot more or a lot less sleep or change in time of day when asleep)	38. _____	16
39.	Major change in number of family get-togethers (e.g., a lot more or a lot less than usual)	39. _____	15
40.	Major change in eating habits (a lot more or a lot less food intake, or very different meal hours or surroundings)	40. _____	15
41.	Vacation	41. _____	13
42.	Christmas	42. _____	12
43.	Minor violations of the law (e.g., traffic tickets, jaywalking, disturbing the peace, etc.)	43. _____	11

Source: Reprinted from the *Journal of Psychosomatic Research, 11*, pp. 213–218, by Holmes and Rahe, "Social Readjustment Rating Scale," © 1967 by Pergamon Press, Ltd., with permission from Elsevier Science.

change are also important. Psychologists have found that when they match two groups, both with LCU totals higher than 300, those who developed physical illnesses had more difficulty in coping emotionally with life changes than did those who did not get sick. Aspects of how you go through your daily life, such as feeling the need to get everything done right on time, also are involved in how you handle potentially troublesome levels of life changes.

This means that after you total your LCUs, you also need to think about how emotionally strong you are to handle those changes and how good your present techniques are for relaxing and easing the pressure.

Your own LCU may suggest a higher—or lower—probability of illness depending on how you deal with stress as it arises. Just being aware of the concept of stress and how life changes increase stress can reduce your own likelihood of getting ill. You can reduce the stress of adjusting to change even further by developing specific techniques, such as relaxation, hobbies, exercise, and meditation.

About the Scale

The most common stress-producing situations in modern life involve fear and frustration. Most people would agree that there is a high degree of stress involved in negative events—such as death of a spouse, marital separation, or going to jail—related to these two emotions. But it took a group of researchers at the University of Washington School of Medicine to point out and quantify that *any* major life change, even a positive one, produces stress. The research team, led by Dr. Thomas Holmes, found in a group of 400 people a high relationship between their amount of life changes during the previous six months and their likelihood of getting sick.

Out of such research came the Life Change Index Scale, which rates 43 life events on the degree of stress each produces. The subsequent research needed to validate the scale is fascinating. The study mentioned earlier involved having 400 people count their LCU over a six-month and one-year period with the researcher then predicting, on the basis of LCU totals, which people would develop a major health problem during the next six months. Another study measured LCU totals in a group of 2,684 Navy and Marine personnel getting ready for a six-month cruise and predicted which people would need the most visits to sick bay during the cruise. Yet another research project involved predicting football injuries during a season on the basis of LCU totals for team members before the season began. In each of these studies, plus numerous others, LCU totals were highly related to the likelihood of any specific person developing a major health problem.

As you look over the events, you will notice that an event such as marital separation produces more stress than does a personal illness or injury. But the positive change of getting back together, marital reconciliation, produces more stress than does a situation involving sex difficulties. Dr. Holmes and his colleagues were among the first researchers to quantify what stress expert Dr. Hans Selye had said for several years, that we must watch out for the impact of positive life changes as well as of those that are clearly negative. As Drs. Holmes and Masuda wrote, "If it takes too much effort to cope with the environment, we have less to spare for preventing disease. When life is too hectic and when coping attempts fail, illness is the unhappy result."

Communicating Effectively with Those in Crisis

What Is the Crisis?

The discussion in Chapter 1 began with a basic question: "WHAT IS A CRISIS?" Moving forward to Chapter 3, the discussion shifts from the general "A CRISIS" to the particular "THE CRISIS." "WHAT IS THE CRISIS?" What happened and how does the victim perceive the event or series of events? What is it about the event that has overwhelmed the victim's usual coping mechanisms? The authors have observed well-intentioned seasoned as well as novice interveners attempt to muddle through an intervention without ever identifying or addressing the actual crisis situation. The intervener failed to ask for information or did not deal with key information provided. The intervener and the victim did not establish a connection and ultimately the sessions ended in frustration and disappointment for all involved. The following vignette illustrates the point:

> INTERVENER: *I see that you are limping. Are you all right?*
> D.B.: *Well, I fell when I was getting the mail yesterday. I'm a little sore.*
> INTERVENER: *I'm sorry. Can I help you?*
> D.B.: *I got an eviction notice yesterday and my ex-husband is taking me to court again for child custody.*
> INTERVENER: *You really have a lot going on.*
> D.B.: *Yes, I have a lot more stuff going on . . . a lot more. . . . And I really don't know what to do. I just don't know. . . . And I don't know if I care.*
> INTERVENER: *Well, why don't we talk about your leg first. I think that's a good start.*
> D.B.: *The problem is not my leg! You are not listening to me. . . . This is a waste of time. I'm leaving.*

D.B. left abruptly. During their verbal transaction, D.B. gave the intervener three important clues about her situation: "I have a lot more stuff going on"; "I just don't know what to do"; "I don't know if I care." Had the intervener gently asked for clarification of those statements, D.B. would have complied. The intervener would have learned that the recent death of D.B.'s father left her bereft of her only trusted advisor and confidant. She feels isolated, desperately lonely, lost. D.B. was looking to the intervener to provide structure in her world, which seemed to her to be falling apart.

WHAT IS THE CRISIS: D.B. was not prepared for the unusual and unexpected feelings of fear and anxiety triggered by her father's death. The realization that she now has total responsibility for herself has immobilized her. She is stuck.

Before a problem can be managed, the intervener must determine what the problem is. Often, more than one problem will be present in a situation. When this occurs, the following nine questions may be asked to determine the priority for intervention.

1. What is troubling the victim now?
2. Why did the victim go into crisis at this particular time?
3. Which problem among the several that may be present is of most immediate concern?
4. Which problem would prove most damaging if not treated immediately?
5. Which problem must be dealt with first before others can be solved?
6. Which problem can be most quickly resolved?
7. What resources for handling problems are available?
8. What variables will hinder the problem-solving process?
9. How can the responder/intervener implement the most effective help in the shortest amount of time?[1]

Although it is necessary to answer all the preceding questions, if the intervener is to help manage the victim's crisis, the intervener must be able to acquire the needed information quickly and accurately. This means that the intervener must listen actively to the victim's total message and give the person full concentration and undivided attention. Further, the intervener must sift through the victim's words and behavior to gain

---

1 The above list is from *Emotional First Aid* by E. S. Rosenbluh. Copyright ©1981 by Rosenbluh. This and all other quotes from the same source are reprinted with permission. Dr. E. S. Rosenbluh.

information and insight into the person's problems and views of those problems. Do not underestimate the value of observing nonverbal behavior. Crisis communication can be both loud and silent. The intervener must be observant and prepared to respond to both. Noise is easier to hear and so it receives more attention. But a victim's glazed over eyes or hollow stare, or his gradual turning of his shoulder away from the intervener, or an obvious mismatch of the victim's words and her demeanor should not be missed or dismissed as being irrelevant.

Every communication from the crisis victim contains three messages: a content message, a feeling message, and a meaning message. The content message provides information about what the sender believes, thinks, or perceives the situation to be. The feeling message conveys the nature and intensity of the sender's emotion about the situation. The meaning message concerns the behavior or situation that has generated the feeling. Usually the person who sends the communication implies, rather than explicitly states, the behavior or situation that creates the feeling. The intervener must try to infer what the behavior or situation is.

Rosenbluh (1981) explains that during the communication between the intervener and the victim, distortion can occur in three areas:

1. What the other person means to say
2. What the other person actually says
3. What the intervener believes he or she hears

The present discussion is concerned with what interveners think they hear. The key to effective listening is accurately hearing the feeling and meaning behind the content of communication. The skill discussed here is empathy. Empathy is one's ability to enter the other person's world and to reflect this understanding to the person. Empathy, as Rosenbluh (1981) points out, contains two elements:

- *Passive empathy*: The ability to hear the facts contained in the words and the feelings contained in the other person's body language, intensity, and tone.
- *Active empathy*: The ability to reflect this understanding to the other person in a manner that generates warmth, trust, and a willingness to be open. This is often a difficult skill for responders. The tendency is to deal only with surface facts. Not penetrating the surface may feel safer and more comfortable and less messy. However, not being able to get below the surface of these facts will reduce the effectiveness of the intervener in assisting the victim. Practice. Practice. Practice and develop the skill.

Mistaken Assumption: "I Know Exactly How You Feel." Even under the best conditions, this is doubtful. If you say you know and you really do not, your credibility as an intervener is destroyed. If you make such a statement to a victim, be prepared to back it up with accurate information about the sufferer's feelings. Making assumptions about the sufferer's feelings too early in the intervention can prove disastrous. Victims of a crisis often want to talk to someone, but they will not talk indiscriminately. Being in crisis does not preclude testing the sincerity of those who say they want to help. The victim can challenge your assumption by saying, "OK, how do I feel?" or "How can you know how I feel? We just met!" The unprepared intervener might have to do some fast backpedaling. Begin with an apology: "I am sorry. I can't know exactly what you're feeling unless you tell me. Would you share . . . " or "How did that make you feel when . . . " Examples of effective responses accompany the vignettes presented throughout the chapter.

Words Do Matter

Effective interveners understand that words have the potential to calm or incite, to empower or diminish, to provide clarity or create confusion, to open up or close down the flow of information, and to enhance or sabotage the process of assisting the victim regain a sense of equilibrium and structure.

Words do matter. An intervener who might think, "I will just say that and see what happens" is courting disaster. It is an attitude that breeches the trust and perhaps the safety of a person who is already in a fragile way. The responsible intervener chooses and uses words carefully, thoughtfully, and purposefully.

What follows are several vignettes. They are included to illustrate effective and ineffective use of words. "I" represents the Intervener; the other initials are those of the victim.

J.K.: *I'm an old, tired woman. I've outlived my children. I've outlived my usefulness.*
INTERVENER: *What about your friends?*
J.K.: *I have to go to the graveyard to see them.*
INTERVENER: *I am sorry for all of your losses, Mrs. K.*
J.K.: *I just don't want to do this anymore. Enough is enough.*
INTERVENER: *What is it that you don't want to do?*

J.K.: *I don't want to bother with life. It's too much trouble. Too much trouble . . .*

INTERVENER: *Is there something that you do want to do? Maybe something you haven't been able to do or see in a long time?*

J.K.: *Well I always liked card games. I liked the challenge. It made me feel alive.*

INTERVENER: *Card games. . . . Do you drive, Mrs. K.?*

J.K.: *I drive to the grocery store. And the doctor sometimes.*

INTERVENER: *Do you mind if I look at your driver's license?*

J.K.: *Am I in trouble?*

INTERVENER (SMILING): *No, I'm looking because I care about your safety. By the way there is a very nice community center at 301 Main Street (reaching into his pocket). This card has their phone number and address. I would like you to call them and ask about their card games. If you don't mind, I will sit right here while you make the call. Then you can tell me all about what you find out. We'll talk some more if you like.*

J.K.: *It's been a long, long time since anybody's cared about me. How about a cup of tea after I call?*

INTERVENER: *Can you tell me what happened in the last twelve hours, Mr. B.?*

M.B.: *Yes, I can tell you. I was laid off again.*

INTERVENER: *Is that good or bad for you?*

M.B.: *Are you crazy? How can it be good? You must be nuts or getting a big share of taxpayers' money so you don't know about being poor.*

INTERVENER: *Look, man . . .*

M.B.: *Don't "look man" me. I got a wife and two kids to support. We bought a house so my mother-in-law could live with us. . . . I can't support all those people now.*

INTERVENER: *What are you most concerned about now?*

M.B.: *I don't have a job. I can't pay my bills. I'm going to lose everything.*

INTERVENER: *I hear your concerns. I'm sorry about my poor attempt at humor. It was a joke I once heard. You said you were laid off before. How did you handle things when that happened?*

M.B.: *The economy was better then. My old company gave us some leads. I didn't have as many bills, so it wasn't so bad. This really scares me. I have never been scared like this before. I don't know what to do, and I don't know how to figure it out.*

INTERVENER: *What you told me is plenty. But is there anything else that you haven't told me? Any other concern?*

M.B.: *I . . . I. . . .I don't even know how to admit this. I am just plain embarrassed. I feel humiliated that I can't support my family. And to have my mother-in-law know I can't support her daughter— That is probably the worst part of all this.*

INTERVENER: *It sounds like you care a lot about your family and do your best for them. Have you talked with your wife?*

M.B.: *I haven't even told her.*

INTERVENER: *What do you think will happen when you tell her?*

M.B. (DEEP BREATH): *You know, probably nothing bad. She's a good person.*

INTERVENER: *Sounds like you both are. How about giving her a chance to show her support. This is a family matter isn't it?*

M.B.: *I guess I hadn't thought of it like that before.*

INTERVENER: *Is there more you want to talk about?*

M.B.: *I can breathe better. I feel some relief. I would like to go home and talk with my wife.*

INTERVENER: *You're a lawyer aren't you, Larry?*

L.L.: *Yes.*

INTERVENER: *How could you get yourself in such a mess?*

INTERVENER: *You're supposed to be the expert in the family, Joe.*

J.: *(no response)*

INTERVENER: *Even I would have known how to handle that.*

J.: *(no response)*

INTERVENER: *I think you should contact your mother, Mary.*

M.: *I told you not to talk about my mother. You are really pushing my buttons and I don't like it.*

INTERVENER: *I am sorry, Mary.*

M.: *Don't tell me you're sorry. You keep doing it!*

INTERVENER: *You had a golden opportunity. What were you thinking about?*

T.: *(no response)*

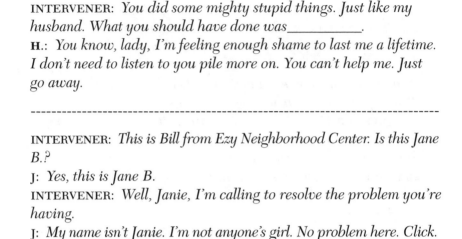

INTERVENER: *You did some mighty stupid things. Just like my husband. What you should have done was_____.*

H.: *You know, lady, I'm feeling enough shame to last me a lifetime. I don't need to listen to you pile more on. You can't help me. Just go away.*

INTERVENER: *This is Bill from Ezy Neighborhood Center. Is this Jane B.?*

J: *Yes, this is Jane B.*

INTERVENER: *Well, Janie, I'm calling to resolve the problem you're having.*

J: *My name isn't Janie. I'm not anyone's girl. No problem here. Click.*

The first two situations were effectively managed. The last several vignettes showed how the intervener's effectiveness can be impaired by the use of sarcasm, preaching, shaming, and editorializing. These interveners will have a difficult time creating trust with the victims. They have compromised the integrity of the intervention process in the service of their own agenda.

Please refer back to the first two vignettes. For Mrs. K the crisis was not a wish for death; it was an unfulfilled longing for human contact and involvement. For M.B. the crisis was not the job loss, but the overwhelming sense of humiliation that accompanied the job loss. What Is THE CRISIS? Attach this question to your Crisis Intervention notebook.

Helpful Phrases to Get Unstuck

There are times during an intervention when the intervener may not know what to ask or how to ask the victim for information. The following is presented as a resource:

...I hear your pain/concern/fear/frustration.
...Help me understand.
...This is what I am hearing. Is that what you meant to say?
...Tell me more about that.
...Could you elaborate on that?
...No. I don't know exactly how you feel, but I am trying to understand more about your feelings/concerns.

...It's important to me because it's obviously important to you.

...Is there anything else?

...Have you ever had that feeling before? How did you handle it then?

...What are you feeling?

...Would you share what you are thinking?

...It is important that I understand what you are telling me. Would you clarify for me?

...Talk to me . . . (use a soft voice)

...Where are you now?

...What if . . . ?

...Are you aware that every time you . . . ?

...Have you ever thought about what might happen if . . . ?

...Something does not feel right about this. What is really going on? or What is really concerning/scaring/worrying/angering you? (These questions are attempts at tuning in to the person without becoming threatening. The person can always back away and the intervener can apologize for misreading them.)

...Let's take a look at . . .

...mmm, hum, yes

...When you tried that what happened?

...Was that helpful?

...What is the worst thing that could happen?

...What is the best thing that could happen?

...When you think about that what do you feel?

...What will you gain?

...What will you lose?

...What need does that serve?

...Has that worked for you before?

...Is it working well for you now?

...What do you need from me right now?

...How can I be helpful to you now?

...Of all your concerns what is the most pressing?

...It sounds like . . .

...Let's take one thing at a time.

...How about "trying on" that idea? You are not wed to it. Just say it out loud.

...How does that idea/plan sound to you?

...We are trying to generate some options. What might work for you?

...Just take baby steps. One step at a time.

...We will figure this out. You are doing well.

....You say you don't know. If you did know, what would your answer be? (this phrase does work)

MISTAKEN ASSUMPTION: "Listening to and Acknowledging Feelings Implies That I Agree With the Victim and the Victim's Behavior"

Relationships are not built on agreement; they are built on understanding. Serious disagreements can exist within a close personal relationship if both parties know that each will take the time to understand the other. Similarly, with a person in crisis it is possible to listen and respond to feelings even though you do not agree with the person's actions. In fact, sometimes you may need to tell the person about your nonagreement. This honesty will not interfere with the relationship building necessary to the intervention or subsequent referral. Rather, the relationship could gain further strength because of your ability to differentiate between feelings and agreement. Also, remember that victims' asking for agreement with their actions can be a way of testing the intervener's sincerity and honesty. The intervener's credibility is at issue here.

Clarification

Sometimes a victim will make a statement that the intervener does not fully understand. At other times, the victim's words and nonverbal behavior may not agree. At that point, the intervener must focus on the misunderstanding and try to clarify the statement before continuing with the intervention. Interveners must never assume that they understand what the victim means. The intervener must find out and know what the victim means. Two people can witness the same event and describe it very differently. Conversely, two people can have very different experiences and relate these experiences similarly. Interveners must be sure they know precisely what the victim is talking about. To do so, the intervener must press the sufferer to clarify vague or ambiguous statements. An intervener cannot work effectively with a victim unless both the intervener and the victim are talking about the same crisis.

Clarification Techniques

Interveners can use the following four techniques to help victims clarify their statements:

1. *Repeating key words.* Using this technique, the intervener repeats key words or phrases that the victim uses and that the intervener does not clearly understand. By emphasizing a certain word or phrase, the intervener focuses attention on a particular thought or feeling and encourages the victim to explain it in more detail.

For example:

VICTIM: *I feel helpless when I think of all these bills . . . and I have no income.*
INTERVENER: *Helpless?*
VICTIM: *I just don't care anymore. I feel so isolated and depressed.*
INTERVENER: *You don't care anymore? (or You feel isolated? or You feel depressed?)*

Interveners should use this technique carefully. When used too frequently, repeating what the person just said can sound like a gimmick. The intervener's parroting could make the victim distrustful and uneasy. Repetition is, however, a useful tool when used cautiously.

1. Restatement. The intervener can rephrase the victim's statements in such a way that the person is encouraged to clarify what was said.

For example:

VICTIM: *I'm behind in all my bills, and my father, who is a local banker, told me it was embarrassing him because my creditors have been calling him, too.*
INTERVENER: *So you're having financial problems, and you are feeling heavy family pressure to find a solution.*

When an intervener uses restatement, the victim will often respond by talking about the most pressing area of concern. Using restatement also encourages the victim to explain the situation in more detail. This additional information will help the intervener understand what the victim is thinking and feeling.

1. Direct method. Perhaps the most direct method of eliciting information is for interveners to admit that they are confused

or puzzled about the victim's statement and to ask the victim for clarification so that better understanding will result. This technique has the added advantage of letting the victim know that the intervener is interested in what is being said. In addition, this kind of communication helps build trust in the intervener-victim relationship.

2. Asking questions. An intervener can obtain a clearer idea of the other person's meaning simply by asking questions. When interveners want more information, they can ask "open" questions. To pinpoint specific items, interveners can ask "closed" questions. A closed question can be answered with a simple "yes" or "no." An open question allows for amplification of meaning by the respondent.

For example:

VICTIM: *I don't know what my husband is talking about.*
INTERVENER: *What does he say that you don't understand?* [open question]
VICTIM: *All I want is the best for my child. I am so miserable and feel so defeated that I want to kill myself.*
INTERVENER: *How would killing yourself help your child?* [open question]
Or
Do you have a suicide plan in mind? [closed question]

The closed-question technique is particularly useful when an intervener is fairly sure of what additional information is needed.

Identifying the victim's concerns during the assessment and attempting to clarify the real issues involved help both the victim and the intervener better understand the total situation that must be dealt with.

Using Questions Effectively

Asking questions to obtain accurate information in an intervention is both necessary and helpful. The intervener must be careful, however, to pace the questions carefully to avoid increasing the victim's stress level. Bombarding victims with a series of questions could confuse and frustrate them. Also, allow sufficient time for the victim to answer. Ask the questions in a nonthreatening, nonaccusatory tone.

Dealing with Silence

The intervener should know how to use silence during an intervention. For some interveners, silence is deadly. It may seem as if nothing is happening, and this can cause the intervener great discomfort. Interveners should handle silence by being silent themselves while observing the victim's behavior and what the victim is not saying.

Responding Effectively

Responding to another person's feelings is a delicate process. In gathering information from victims, the intervener must handle the victims' feelings with care and concern. If the intervener wants a victim to continue talking about facts pertinent to the problem, the intervener cannot judge, use logic, or give advice. The individual's feelings must be legitimized. The following example illustrates ineffective response to emotions:

> BOY: *I can't stand my father. He's been mean to me all my life.*
> INTERVENER: *That's unfair. What would you do if anything happened to him? You'd feel awful to have said things like that.*

In this instance, communication has been effectively shut off. The intervener has passed judgment and shamed the boy instead of seeking the root of the hostility. Here is another way to handle this situation:

> BOY: *I can't stand my father. He's been mean to me all my life.*
> INTERVENER: *Has your father done something mean recently?*
> BOY: *Yes.*
> INTERVENER: *Would you tell me about that?*
> BOY: *He wouldn't let me go to the game with my friends. I had to work.*
> INTERVENER: *That upset you.*
> BOY: *I just want to smash something. It's unfair. Everybody else got to go.*
> INTERVENER: *What kind of work did you do?*
> BOY: *All kinds of stuff that I was supposed to do last week.*
> INTERVENER: *I'd like to hear about it.*

Mistaken Assumption: "If You Can't Help Them, At Least Don't Hurt Them"

The assumption here is that there can be a "non effect" of intervention on the sufferer. This is not so. When a person intervenes in another person's crisis, that person will either be helped or hurt as a result of the intervention. Under no circumstances will the sufferer be unaffected. The effect, whether positive or negative, will be determined by what the intervener does or does not do. Therefore, knowing when to stay out is as important as knowing when to become involved. There is no shame in not intervening if you decide your skills are inadequate in a particular situation or that your own psychological well-being is at stake. If you decide to intervene in a situation that you cannot handle, however, your involvement will worsen the situation. Your decision to intervene requires you to accept that your action will have some direct, important impact on the person in crisis.

Guidelines for Effective Communications in Crises

1. Listen effectively.
   - Fully hear what the other person is saying.
   - Maintain eye contact if at all possible.
   - Let the other person talk freely.
   - Try to comprehend what the other person is saying.
   - Listen for both feelings and content.
   - Paraphrase the other's statements to gain clarification.
   - Ask for clarification when necessary.
   - Don't let your own feelings get in the way of understanding what the other person is trying to say.
2. Respond descriptively.
   - Don't be evaluative in your response; evaluative statements tend to elicit defensiveness.
   - Keep in mind that "rightness" or "wrongness" might not be the issue.
   - Remember, effective communication is not a contest; a "win or lose" mentality is inappropriate.
   - Learn all you can about the other person's thoughts and feelings.
   - Use descriptive statements and reveal your reactions to the other person.
3. Use your own feelings.
   - Remember that feelings are important in communicating and that they are always present.

- Practice expressing your feeling.
- Take responsibility for your feelings.
- Use "I" messages rather than "you" messages; "I" messages reduce threat to the other person.
- Use descriptive statements that contain feelings.
- Be clear and specific about your feelings.

4. Assess needs.
   - Consider the needs of all involved.
   - Address issues over which the victim has actual control.
   - Avoid being judgmental and critical; avoid preaching.

5. Make timely responses.
   - Deliver responses at the time they are most important.
   - Deliver responses as soon as possible after the behavior that requires response.
   - Do not store up old concerns for later discussion.
   - Do not use old or saved concerns as a weapon.
   - Assess whether the other person is ready to handle your responses at this time.
   - Consider delaying responses on sensitive issues until you are in a more appropriate setting.
   - Discuss emotional issues in private.
   - Practice communication skills for greatest effectiveness.

Listening

During conversation with victims, keep in mind the following items about the importance of listening:

1. Listening is basic to successful communications.
2. Listening requires responsiveness.
3. Listening enables the listener to know more about the speaker.
4. Listening encourages expression.
5. Listening allows exploration of both feelings and content.
6. Listening helps establish trust between the parties.
7. Listening allows greater accuracy of communication.
8. Listening requires practice and is not always easy to learn.
9. Listening includes listening for content, feelings, and point of view.

10. Listening lets the speaker relax.
11. Listening enables the listener to watch for attitudes and feelings that might be conveyed nonverbally.

When you listen, remember to do the following:

1. Attend to verbal content.
2. Attend to nonverbal cues.
3. Hear and observe.
4. Attend to the feelings expressed by the speaker.
5. Don't think about other things when you are listening to someone.
6. Don't listen with only "half an ear."
7. Become attuned to the speaker's verbal and nonverbal messages.
8. Note any extra emphasis the speaker places on certain words.
9. Notice the speaker's speech patterns and recurring themes.

Nonverbal Communications

The following are examples of nonverbal acts a speaker may use to communicate:

- Sighing
- Flipping through papers
- Wincing
- Looking around, up, or down
- Smoking
- Chewing gum
- Yawning
- Tapping a finger or foot
- Frowning
- Displaying nervousness
- Avoiding eye contact
- Saying nothing
- Making jerky gestures
- Dressing sloppily
- Blinking rapidly
- Constantly looking at a clock or watch
- Showing favoritism

- Acting bored
- Being drunk

Certain nonverbal cues can indicate a specific attitude. Some examples follow.

NONVERBAL CUES THAT CAN INDICATE OPENNESS

- Uncrossed legs
- Open hands
- Unbuttoned coat, or unbuttoning the coat
- Hands spread apart
- Palms up
- Leaning forward

NONVERBAL CUES THAT CAN INDICATE DEFENSIVENESS

- Fists closed
- Arms crossed in front of individual
- Legs crossed
- One leg over the chair arm

NONVERBAL CUES THAT CAN INDICATE COOPERATION

- Opening coat
- Head tilted
- Sitting on the edge of a chair
- Eye contact
- Hand-to-face gestures
- Leaning forward

NONVERBAL CUES THAT CAN INDICATE EVALUATING

- Head tilted
- Chin stroking
- Looking over glasses
- Pacing
- Pinching the bridge of the nose

NONVERBAL CUES THAT CAN INDICATE READINESS

- Hands on hips
- Leaning

- Confident speech
- Moving closer to the other person

NONVERBAL CUES THAT CAN INDICATE SUSPICION

- Lack of eye contact
- Glancing sideways at the other person
- Body apparently pointed toward exit from area
- Touching the bridge of the nose
- Rubbing the ears
- Rubbing the eyes

NONVERBAL CUES THAT CAN INDICATE CONFIDENCE

- Elevating oneself by sitting on a higher chair or standing on a platform
- Finger "steepling"
- Hands clasped behind the back
- Feet on a desk or table
- Leaning on an object
- Clucking sound
- Leaning back, with both hands supporting the neck

Both the following list and Figure 3.1 are guides that an intervener can show to victims who are having trouble identifying their feelings.

Feelings That Persons Have But Often Fail to Identify

Abandoned	Bored	Contented
Adequate	Brave	Cruel
Affectionate	Calm	Crushed
Ambivalent	Capable	Deceitful
Angry	Challenged	Defeated
Annoyed	Charmed	Delighted
Anxious	Cheated	Desirous
Apathetic	Cheerful	Despair
Astounded	Childish	Destructive
Awed	Clever	Determined
Bad	Combative	Different
Betrayed	Competitive	Disappointed
Bitter	Condemned	Discontented
Blissful	Confused	Distraught
Bold	Conspicuous	Disturbed

Divided	Infatuated	Pressured
Dominated	Infuriated	Proud
Eager	Inspired	Quarrelsome
Ecstatic	Intimidated	Rage
Embarrassed	Irritated	Refreshed
Empty	Isolated	Rejected
Enchanted	Jealousy	Relaxed
Energetic	Joyous	Relieved
Enjoyment	Jumpy	Remorse
Envious	Kind	Restless
Evil	Lazy	Righteous
Exasperated	Lecherous	Sad
Excited	Left out	Sated
Exhausted	Lonely	Satisfied
Fascinated	Longing	Scared
Fearful	Love	Screwed up
Flustered	Loving	Sexy
Foolish	Low	Shocked
Frantic	Lustful	Silly
Free	Mad	Skeptical
Frightened	Mean	Sneaky
Frustrated	Miserable	Solemn
Furious	Mystical	Sorrowful
Glad	Naughty	Spiteful
Good	Nervous	Startled
Gratified	Nice	Stingy
Greedy	Nutty	Stuffed
Grief Guilty	Obnoxious	Stupid
Happy Hate	Obsessed	Stunned
Heavenly	Odd	Suffering
Helpful	Outraged	Sure
Helpless	Overwhelmed	Sympathetic
High	Pain	Talkative
Homesick	Panicked	Tempted
Horrible	Peaceful	Tense
Hurt	Persecuted	Terrible
Hysterical	Petrified	Terrified
Ignored	Pity	Threatened
Imposed upon	Pleasant	Tired
Impressed	Pleased	Trapped

Troubled   Violent   Weepy
Ugly   Vehement   Wicked
Uneasy   Vulnerable   Wonderful
Unsettled   Vivacious   Worried

AGGRESSIVE   ANXIOUS   APOLOGETIC   ARROGANT   BLISSFUL

BORED   CONFIDENT   ECSTATIC   ENRAGED   EXASPERATED

EXHAUSTED   FRUSTRATED   GUILTY   HUNGOVER   HYSTERICAL

INDIFFERENT   INNOCENT   INTERESTED   LOADED   LONELY

LOVESTRUCK   MEDITATIVE   MISERABLE   NEGATIVE   OPTIMISTIC

SATISFIED   SURLY   TURNED-ON   TURNED-OFF   WITHDRAWN

FIGURE 3.1
How Do You Feel Today?

Team Intervention

Team Intervention Responsibilities and Procedures

Although many crisis situations can be effectively handled by a single intervener, some circumstances dictate the use of a team of interveners or multiple teams of interveners. The importance of the team concept rests in its potential for providing maximum safety for all involved, for efficient information gathering from the crisis victims, for division of responsibility among the team members, and for emotional and physical support for the team members. Effective team intervention requires that each team member accept personal responsibility for his or her share of the team effort. Failure to acknowledge and assume this responsibility could exacerbate the crisis and jeopardize the safety of the other team members. Because of the number of people being managed (both victims and interveners), team interventions must be carefully and thoughtfully orchestrated. This chapter deals with the designation and role of lead teams and lead interveners, the division of responsibility of the interveners, and the positioning of the team members as part of the Crisis Intervention procedure.

Crisis Intervention can be done by a single intervener, a team of interveners, or multiple teams of interveners (see Figure 4.1). The decision to use a single intervener, a team, or multiple teams will be dictated by the number of crisis victims involved in the particular situation and the nature of the situation. The greater the number of victims and the more potentially hostile the circumstance is, the greater the need is for the control and safety backup that multiple teams can offer. A family dispute involving two members might require a team intervention. A large family dispute involving significant others might necessitate multiple teams. A dispute between two students might be handled effectively by a single intervener or by a team. A playground dispute involving the primary victims, bystanders, hecklers, and other agitators will require multiple teams.

Effective intervention in a crisis situation requires that an intervener be emotionally and physically prepared to intervene in the situation at hand. The intervener must ask several important questions in determining his or her readiness. These questions include the following:

1. Is this an intervention that I can emotionally and physically handle?
2. Will personal, unresolved biases or prejudices interfere with my ability to be effective? (The most blatant example of bias often exists in child abuse cases, where the intervener might not be willing to acknowledge the crisis being experienced by the abuser and might focus only on the crisis of the child. This attitude can potentiate crisis for the intervener and increase the stress level of those already in crisis.)

Single intervener intervention

Single team intervention

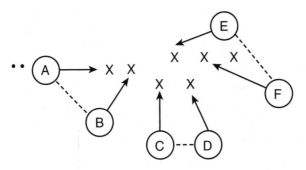

Multiple team intervention

FIGURE 4.1
A,B,C,D,E,F = Crisis Interveners
X's = Victims
------- = Team Relationships
•• = Control or Lead Intervener

3. Will my physical safety be in jeopardy if I intervene in this situation? Do we need additional support personnel before we enter the situation?
4. Is the line of communication between my partner and me fail-safe?
5. Can I depend on my partner?

The intervener who experiences ambiguity in the answers and is unwilling to resolve the problems immediately risks sabotaging his or her effectiveness and putting him or herself and the partner in danger. Lack of clarity could exacerbate the suffering of the victims and also cause the intervener to go into crisis.

If, however, the intervener and partner are clear about their goal, reasonably certain of their safety, in agreement on team procedure, and prepared to intervene regardless of the situation, then they should proceed with the intervention.

While team and multiple team interventions follow the six basic steps of Crisis Intervention procedure—(1) immediacy, (2) control, (3) assessment, (4) disposition, (5) referral, and (6) follow-up—team members have specific responsibilities inherent in the team structure.

The following is an outline of the procedure and the team members' responsibilities within the procedure.

Immediacy

Intervention Procedure In approaching a crisis, the immediacy of the intervention is vital. The team must attempt to relieve anxiety, prevent further disorientation, and ensure that the victims do not harm themselves or others.

Control

Intervention Procedure The necessity for adequate situational controls differs little from that needed in any type of Crisis Intervention attempt. The additional factors in a team approach are related to the number of victims involved, the increased possibility of hostility, the group dynamics, and the increase in the amount of information that must be received and understood by the interveners. Proper control procedures protect the victims of crisis, the interveners, significant others, and bystanders and assist in defusing the high-pitched emotional tone present in almost all crises.

RESPONSIBILITIES OF TEAM MEMBERS

1. Team A is the lead team. Intervener A is the lead intervener.
2. Decide before entering the crisis situation which team member will intervene with which victim. Time is limited. The decision must be made quickly and on the basis of on-the-spot assessment and past experience. Often the interveners' skills and experience in the particular situation determine the pairing. Regardless of how the designation is made, the interveners must follow the game plan. A faltering entrance, with interveners unsure of their positions, will cause additional confusion and chaos.
3. The teams must give an impression of structure.
4. In multiple interventions, Team A will enter first and begin the intervention process with the designated victims. Team B will observe and assess the situation, then move in at the direction of its team leader. The goal of Team B is to complement and support Team A's effort, not compete with the process already begun. Team C will move in as appropriate.
5. If it seems prudent for the interveners to switch victims, eye signals and hand signals may be used to direct the switch. This strategy can be done effectively if eye contact between the interveners is maintained.
6. The Team A leader must carefully assess the situation before deciding to make a switch. If Team B members have gained control and begun establishing rapport with their victims, it is counterproductive to interrupt the process. The bottom line is always a commitment to the needs and concerns of the victims, not to technique gimmickry.
7. Avoid leaving victims unattended. Being left alone increases the possibility of the victims renewing the conflict, harming themselves or others, or feeling helpless and isolated again. Interveners must maintain the trust of the victims.

8. All teams must be prepared for the unexpected. When emotions are charged, behavior is often unpredictable. When numerous people are involved, one person's irrational act can trigger a domino effect. A sudden flare-up or new crisis can occur at any point during the intervention. The teams must be aware of this possibility and be ready to respond. This might require reintervening or starting over again to gain control, and then moving to the assessment process. The team's calm self-control and patience will mean the difference between reducing the stress and tension and exacerbating the new crisis. This underscores the need for team members and member teams to remain in contact and to know where each team is positioned. Such emotional and physical support translates into intervener survival as well as into effective intervention.

9. In a situation involving large numbers, team leaders should identify the victim who requires the most urgent attention and begin intervening with him or her. Teams B and C will then move in to intervene where necessary.

10. When control has been established, the Team A leader will convene other team leaders to exchange information and to move to the assessment phase.

Assessment

INTERVENTION PROCEDURE

1. The lead intervener A gathers information from the crisis victim, while team member B monitors verbal and nonverbal information. Body language is an important source of information and should be noted.

2. When necessary, team member B asks for further information to clarify what has been said.

3. As appropriate, team member B intervenes separately with a victim. For example, in a family dispute it is often prudent to intervene with a young child or children separately from the other family members so the intervener can establish rapport with the child or children. Interveners often make the mistake of excluding children from the intervention process even when the problem centers on them, or when they are in crisis

themselves. It is often assumed that children who are not crying, who are not visibly upset, or who do not request help must be handling the situation like "big people." By attending to children during the crisis period, the intervener will help effectively manage problems that might otherwise continue to surface throughout their adulthoods. For a variety of reasons, including intimidation, ambivalent loyalties, and confusion, children might not be willing to express themselves in the family group. In a one-on-one situation, a sensitive, caring intervener can help children articulate pressing problems.

4. A family crisis situation may involve significant others such as grandparents, in-laws, or other relatives who are present when the interveners arrive at the scene. As appropriate, intervener B can intervene with significant others, either within the room or in a separate area of the room.

5. If the group is large, the primary team may find it necessary to bring in another team. Disputes on a school yard, a crisis in a shopping center, and disputes during an athletic event will all attract and involve large numbers of people. A single intervener might need additional backup to maintain control and to intervene effectively.

6. During the assessment, the team members will confer to share information and to determine an appropriate time to bring the disputants or victims together again.

RESPONSIBILITIES OF TEAM MEMBERS

1. Maintain eye contact with each other to ensure mutual protection.

2. Have clearly defined signals concerning caucusing and switching victims.

3. Have a clearly defined understanding of individual roles before entering the situation. Competition, hidden agendas, and power plays among interveners will sabotage an intervention. There must be clarity of rules and a unity of purpose if the intervention is to be effective. Generally, the lead intervener is designated by mutual consent of the team; the lead team is the first team on the scene. Any changes made during the intervention process must be arranged carefully and smoothly to avoid confusion and or escalating the crisis.

4. Avoid interrupting the other interveners or the victims.
5. Avoid crossing a verbal transaction between intervener and victim or introducing a competing idea during a transaction. Crisis victims require structure and clarity. To create additional confusion by asking many questions in rapid succession or by asking conflicting questions is counterproductive. The interveners must listen to each other. Caucus or signal the other team members if their approaches are obviously not helpful.
6. Caucus as appropriate to share information and to develop strategy. The caucus must be brief; a lengthy meeting could renew feelings of isolation, fear, and mistrust in the victim.
7. Identify the nature of the precipitating events. If intervener A is responsible for interviewing both or all victims, intervener B should attend to the information and give feedback to the intervener A. Intervener B should ask for clarification if necessary and generally support the efforts of intervener A.
8. Team members must be reassuring and calm, maintaining a certain steadiness and warmth toward the crisis victims. They must be attentive and empathetic and be willing to reach out to the victims both emotionally and physically if needed.

Disposition

INTERVENTION PROCEDURE

1. In agreement with the other team members, the lead intervener A will bring the victims together to discuss the particular problems that they are experiencing.
2. Lead intervener A will request each victim to articulate the problem as he or she perceives it. Intervener A must insist that that the speaker not be interrupted by the other party or parties.
3. Help the victims develop or reinstitute adaptive coping mechanisms. Help the victims move from maladaptive behavior to more realistic and effective functioning. Help the victims mobilize their own resources and explore options. Crisis victims experience difficulty in perceiving options in their lives. This feeling of being helpless and impotent heightens stress

and ultimately creates the crisis. The intervener must help the victims recognize available, viable options for managing their problems.

4. Intervention teams must try to build a sense of structure that the victims can relate to. The more that the victims understand, and the more that they can begin to secure a sense of control and structure, the sooner they will be able to regain their self-control and function effectively.

RESPONSIBILITIES OF TEAM MEMBERS

1. Seat victims and interveners carefully to create an atmosphere conducive to problem management.
2. Intervener B should support lead intervener A's efforts to maintain control. Minimize interruptions.
3. Do not cross transactions.
4. Clarify and simplify; do not create additional or new confusion.
5. In offering options, allow the victims sufficient time to digest an idea. Avoid battering victims with many ideas in rapid succession. Move slowly and thoughtfully to eliminate confusion or frustration.
6. Learn to be comfortable with silence. Do not prolong the procedure out of a fear that silence might be seen as impotence or lack of interest by the intervener. If lead intervener A is successfully directing the procedure, intervener B should support that effort. Concern, interest, and empathy can be communicated by nonverbal behavior as well as by verbal expression.

Referral

Intervention Procedure The interveners have as their main concerns the immediate crisis problems rather than those that might be chronic and not immediately present. Often, however, the interveners must make a proper referral subsequent to the intervention.

With only a short time to intervene effectively and to discuss referrals, it is important that the team be prepared to make efficient and effective suggestions for additional help where needed.

RESPONSIBILITIES OF TEAM MEMBERS

1. Each member of the team should have an updated referral list of resources that provides correct current addresses, phone numbers, availability of staff, hours of operation, cost of services, qualifications for obtaining services, available transportation to the referral agency, and the name of a contact person at the agency.
2. In consultation, the team members should determine which referral or referrals would be most appropriate under the circumstances.
3. Team leader A should assume responsibility for obtaining a verbal commitment from the victim that he or she will call at a particular time to set up an appointment with the agency. If possible, have the victim make the call while the intervener is present to give support.
4. Team member B should assume responsibility for giving the victim a card or paper with the name, address, phone number, and contact person at the referral agency.

Follow-up

One of the team members should assume responsibility for follow-up to determine if the appointment was made, if the victim kept the appointment, and if there were any problems.

It is strongly suggested that:

1. Teams of interveners should be created within agencies, organizations, schools, hospitals. Smooth team functioning results from the experience of working together and training together.
2. Wherever possible, the intervention teams should establish a method of debriefing within their organization or agency. Having someone available to listen to feelings and concerns is a key to intervener survival. The debriefing can also be used as an opportunity to share new approaches, reinforce ideas, and to strengthen skills.

Special Issues for the Intervener

In the previous chapters, the authors cited two key elements in the delivery of effective crisis intervention: preparation and awareness. It would be difficult to initiate a discussion of safety issues without taking note of and understanding the relationship that exists between safety procedures and personal and situational awareness. It is a given that all crisis situations are not alike. It is also true that interveners develop individual styles in responding to crisis victims. Regardless of the situation and regardless of the intervener's style, the intervener must recognize that the potential for violence exists and that matters of safety and personal well-being must be dealt with as necessary.

Much of what the intervener does in preparing for a session, much of what is done during a session, and even what is done after the session has ended will make a difference in the area of safety. If the concern for safety factors becomes second nature to the intervener, the likelihood of a positive outcome is increased. Begin to orient yourself to a mode of safety consciousness. This consciousness should include concerns for the welfare of the crisis victims, the interveners, and even the office staff in the agency to which you might be attached. The receptionist (and sometimes the maintenance person) is frequently the first to be approached by the victim and should participate in safety training along with the interveners. This is a team effort that requires team support and backup, and everyone needs to be on the same page.

Probably the intervener's best tool to detect potential violence or the presence of weapons is his or her own communication and sensing capabilities. This often unacknowledged asset is called an "inkling." All of us at some time have experienced inklings: partial awarenesses that are not clear or complete in terms of our central awareness. It may be a sense that something is wrong, or that there is more in the room than meets the eye. The successful intervener has developed the use of these sensing devices in the skillful art of intervening and in personal and victim safety.

Develop your sensing capabilities. Fine tune them to give accurate information. Be open to the information that the senses provide. Inklings, intuitions, "gut feelings," hunches, and fear are similar to red-flag alerts.

The following are examples of incidents where inklings were ignored. "I" is intervener. Initial is victim.

I: *When did you know that your marriage would fail?*
M: *After our third date. I realized how controlling he was. But I thought I could fix him. I cried a lot. I knew he was wrong for me. But I loved him. After ten years I still haven't fixed him—*
I: *You loaned him a lot of money. Now you're in financial trouble. Tell me how it happened.*
J: *It didn't feel right, but you know he was my friend since I was a little kid. I was worried, but I thought it was just me and my worrying nature. I worry about everything. And he was my friend. What really bothered me was when he refused to sign a payment plan. Said that was an insult to our friendship. I lent him the money anyway.*
I: *How did you expect it to turn out?*
P: *Just like it did. There were red flags from the beginning.*
INTERVENER TO SUPERVISOR: *I have a little problem.*
SUPERVISOR: *I'm listening.*
I: *I was the intervener in a crisis situation last month. I'm receiving phone calls from the man. Last night I ran into him at the grocery store across the street.*
S: *When did the calls begin?*
I: *Four days after the intervention. The conversations have become more personal and more frequent. His issue was rejection. I'm afraid if I cut him off it will trigger another crisis. I'm getting scared. He has my home phone number and now he knows where I shop. I knew I shouldn't have kept taking those personal calls like I did.*
S: *Someone will cover your next appointment. I would like you to remain in my office, please. You and I will continue this conversation in 15 minutes.*
"I knew I shouldn't have done that but . . . "
"I knew it wouldn't work, but . . . "
"I knew she was right, but . . . "
Intuition is a gift we all have but often do not value or respect.

Safety Procedures

During an intervention, the crisis intervener's safety is a major consideration. The possibility of injury to the intervener exists regardless of professional capacity. For that reason, the authors suggest the following safety procedures. The procedures must be adapted to each individual crisis situation and to the intervener's skill and training.

Out of the Office

1. If possible, always intervene with a partner. This is especially important when there is more than one victim or disputant.
2. Approach the crisis or potential crisis slowly and carefully. If you are approaching a house, building, or room, take time to survey the surroundings for clues that might help later. Although time is critical in Crisis Intervention, the precautions that you take at the outset could prevent problems later.
3. If you are in a car, do not park directly in front of the area where the crisis is occurring. Assess what is happening around you as you leave your vehicle. Be observant at all times.
4. Approach all doors or openings with caution. Do not stand directly in front of doors or windows. Stand to one side, and, only then knock on the door. Interveners have been killed or injured during family disputes by bullets fired through a door in response to the intervener's knock.
5. Before knocking or ringing the doorbell, listen for 10 to 15 seconds for additional clues that could help you as you enter the situation. These could include screaming, objects being broken, weapons being fired, angry voices, or threats. Perhaps you will hear no noise at all.
6. Once the door is opened, maintain control of the situation by keeping everyone involved in front of you and within eyesight.
7. Perform a visual "frisk" of all persons in the room to determine if weapons are hidden in pockets, belts, shoes, and so on. Pay attention!!

8. Observe the persons in crisis. What are they doing? What must you do immediately to stabilize the situation? Do it!!

9. Note any objects in the room that could be used in a violent way. A heavy ashtray or an innocent letter opener could become a lethal weapon in the hands of a violent person.

10. Be aware of all other persons in the room, and note all persons who enter after you arrive. Assume nothing. Observe both the verbal and nonverbal behavior of everyone in the room. Find out who else is in the house and their locations, if possible.

11. Be prepared for unexpected behavior of significant others, neighbors, or visitors in the house.

12. Initially, step into the room only a few feet at a time. Proceed only as far as it seems safe.

13. If necessary separate the disputants. Avoid using the kitchen, bedroom, or bathroom; weapons are often stored in those areas.

14. Gain control as quickly as possible. You may use anything short of physical force, as appropriate and according to your training. A shrill whistle, a loud clap, a loud voice, an absurd request under the circumstances (asking permission to use a phone book, for example), or other attention-getting devices may be used for this purpose.

15. Have the victims sit down. The failure of the crisis victims to sit does not preclude a successful intervention; however, the potential for violence and aggression seems to be lower when everyone is seated.

16. Select an appropriate place to sit so you can maintain your own safety, gain and maintain control of the situation, and proceed with the intervention.

17. Visually assess the room and the adjoining areas, if possible.

18. Know where entrances and exits are.

19. Know where you might get assistance should you need it. Is there a working telephone in the room? Do you have a portable phone, cell phone, or radio? Do you have emergency phone numbers that you might need?

20. Sit in the following manner: feet solidly on the floor with heels and toes touching the floor; hands unfolded in your lap; your

body leaning slightly forward toward the victim. This position accomplishes two important functions:

21. It gives the victim the feeling that you are attentive to what is being said and experienced. Your body language conveys a sense of interest and concern.

22. It permits you to respond immediately should you be physically threatened. Although a crossed-leg, folded-arm, or a similarly relaxed position might be more comfortable, it can reduce your ability to respond quickly should an immediate response be needed.

23. Attempt to speak with the crisis victim at eye level.

24. Avoid standing above the victim in an authoritarian or parental manner. If the victim chooses to remain standing, you should remain standing also.

25. Do not turn your back on a crisis victim or allow the victim to walk behind you.

26. Do not position yourself in a corner from which you cannot exit if necessary.

27. Remove any objects or extraneous clothing parts that a violent victim could use against you. Name tags connected by pins; pens and pencils; regular non-clip on neckties; scarves; and jewelry, such as chain necklaces or hoop earrings; are all potential weapons in the wrong hands.

28. Stand in the following manner: feet placed shoulder-width apart; one foot slightly behind the other; weight on the rear leg; knees slightly bent; hands folded, but not interlocked, on the upper abdomen or lower chest; arms unfolded. This unrestricted stance permits instant response to a physical threat. Hands placed in one's pockets are suspect, and having to remove your hands from your pockets increases your response time. Folded arms can be threatening and can also impede your response time. Maintaining your weight on the rear leg with knees slightly bent permits quick movement in almost any position without affecting balance.

29. Once separated, bring the disputants back as soon as it seems prudent to do so.

30. Maintain eye contact with your partner and attempt to break eye contact between the disputants as soon as possible.

In the Office

In the office, allow for maximum personal safety by doing the following:

1. Remove potential weapons such as heavy ashtrays, paper-weights, letter openers, or scissors.

   a. Arrange seating so that victims have access to the exit without going over you.
   b. When you greet victims, notice anything strange or unusual about their words, actions, or dress. Allow your senses to give you clues, and take all these clues seriously until you have been able to rule them out.
   c. Observe the victims' body language as they enter.
   d. Enter the room behind the victims. Visually "frisk" the victims.
   e. If possible, arrange several seating areas within the room that can be used as needed with different threat levels.
   f. Do not remain after hours with a potentially violent victim unless proper security is available.
   g. Arrange a "buddy system" so that someone is available should you need help.
   h. If you know that the victims are involved in situations where there is a potential for violence, arrange to have a co-intervener with you, or at least close at hand. As appropriate, inform the victim about other persons available.
   i. After hours, enter your office in the same careful manner that you would enter a crisis victim's house.
   j. Enter elevators only after checking for other passengers.
   k. Know your emergency telephone numbers and use them if you need help. Do not hesitate.

2. If at all possible, always intervene with a partner.
3. Make contingency plans for all interventions. Consider what you would do under a variety of conditions. Learn to play the "what if" game! Play it often. Preplanning will affect automatic behavior under stress.
4. Always take safety precautions seriously. The intervention and your life may depend on your behavior in this regard.
5. Checklists to include in the discussion of safety
6. Identifying students at risk for violent behavior

The following checklists of "early warning signs" will aid in identifying students who might need intervention. The more items that are checked, the greater the potential is for violent acting-out behavior.

CHILDREN AND ADOLESCENTS AT RISK MIGHT:

- Express self-destructive or homicidal ideation
- Have a history of self-destructive behavior
- Articulate specific plans to harm self or others
- Engage in "bullying" other children
- Have difficulty with impulse control
- Evidence significant changes in behavior
- Engage in substance abuse
- Become involved with gangs
- Evidence a preoccupation with fighting
- Have a history of antisocial behavior
- Evidence a low tolerance for frustration
- Externalize blame for their difficulties
- Have harmed small animals
- Have engaged in fire setting
- Evidence persistent bed wetting
- Appear to be or acknowledge feeling depressed
- Talk about not being around
- Express feelings of hopelessness
- Give away possessions
- Appear withdrawn
- Evidence significant changes in mood
- Experience sleep and eating disturbances
- Have experienced prior trauma or tragedy
- Have been or are victims of child abuse
- Have experienced a significant loss
- Evidence a preoccupation with television programs or movies with violent themes
- Evidence a preoccupation with guns and other weapons
- Have access to a firearm
- Have brought a weapon to school
- Evidence frequent disciplinary problems
- Exhibit poor academic performance
- Have been frequently truant from school

Reprinted with permission from a *Practical Guide to Crisis Response in our Schools* 1999 by the American Academy of Experts in

Traumatic Stress, 368 Veterans Memorial Highway, Commack, New York 11725.

The American Psychological Association (APA & MTV, 1999) has compiled a list of nine signs that a child is likely to become violent. Each individual factor is important to consider; however, clusters of factors might be more indicative.

APA WARNING SIGNS

- Loss of temper on a daily basis
- Frequent physical fighting
- Significant vandalism or property damage
- Increase in risk-taking behavior
- Detailed plans to commit acts of violence
- Threatening to hurt others
- Enjoy hurting animals
- Carrying a weapon

The American Academy of Child and Adolescent Psychiatry (APA & MTV, 1999) has also developed a list of factors that might help identify at-risk children. Although no set of factors is absolute, all behavior has meaning. Understanding that meaning helps teachers and interveners help students.

AACAP WARNING SIGNS

- Previous aggressive or violent behavior
- Being the victim of physical abuse, sexual abuse, or both
- Exposure to violence in the home or in the community
- Having a parent who is violent
- Heavy exposure to violence on television or in movies
- Use of drugs and alcohol
- Presence of firearms in the home
- Brain damage from head injury

Identifying Adults at Risk for Violent Behavior

The following checklist can give important clues to the potential for violent acts by those under observation. Although there is no single or simplistic answer to the problem, greater awareness of some of the factors involved can help in planning and response to such potential behavior. As the number of factors increase, the likelihood of violence may also increase, even though the type of violent behavior may not be apparent. Observation of only a few factors does not preclude violence. Conversely, multiple factors do not predict with certainty that violence is imminent.

- Historical problems, singular or serial, are severe enough to warrant police intervention.
- The person expresses feelings of powerlessness to effect the outcome of his or her dispute with another.
- The situation experienced by the person is the result of a family dispute or divorce, especially if children are involved.
- There is a history of causing deliberate encounters with the police or confrontations with other authorities relative to a personal case before the court or in relation to orders of the court.
- There is current or historical use of minor children as a tool, pawn, or weapon against the other spouse in a family dispute.
- The conflict experienced involves allegations of child abuse or spouse abuse.
- Where there are allegations of abuse, a complaint has been filed by either or both parties that has been or is about to be presented in court.
- Direct threats have been made from one party against the other or by third parties against either or both parties.
- There is a history of difficult court appearances or ineffective legal battles.
- Persons show an unusual interest in or expenditures of limited personal resources for reforming an inadequate, unfair, unjust judicial, social, professional, or employment system. Such interests or expenditures seem disproportionate to other activities in the person's life.
- The person has a history of recent multiple life stressors either directly related or unrelated to the current conflict experienced.
- The person indicates high levels of personal dissatisfaction with his or her life.
- The cultural background of the actor emphasizes a major importance of "loss of face" or of male dominance in relationships.
- The person has a perceived or actual lack of personal support systems. He or she might be seen as a loner or as interested in non-human interactions.
- The person makes verbalizations concerning homicide or suicide.
- The verbalizations concern "setting affairs in order" or sound like the making of a "verbal will."

- The person has a history of impulsive acts.
- Those observing the person have an intuitive feeling that something is about to happen of a violent nature.
- The person has recently purchased a weapon and ammunition absent a historical interest in such items.
- The person has a history of high interest in weapons coupled with substantial recent purchases of weapons and ammunition.
- The person has a history of perceived or actual multiple personal losses.
- The person has a history of multiple life changes within a relatively short time period.
- The person has a diagnosed psychiatric disorder.
- The person shows inappropriately subdued affect or behavior that is an inconsistent reaction to the actual issues at hand.
- The person has a history of violent acts with animals during childhood.
- The person's developmental history indicates a lack of early, constant, and nurturing attachments.
- The person grew up within an impulsive family structure or in an overly controlled family.
- Violence in person's family of orientation is seen as a mode of communication.
- The peer group of the subject endorses violence.
- The person has a history of or current job instability.
- The person has a medical history of central nervous system trauma or current subjective CNS symptoms such as complaints of dizziness, blackouts, amnesia, memory loss, headaches, nausea, episodic rage, or sense of confusion with remorse.
- The person shows objective central nervous system signs.
- The person expresses the need to "get even with them."

Pre-Incident Indicators Associated with Spousal/Partner Violence

There are many reliable pre-incident indicators associated with spousal/partner/date/acquaintance violence. The list is not exhaustive, and those indicators listed will not all be present in every case. If a situation has several of these signals, there is a reason for concern.

- The woman has intuitive feelings that she is at risk.
- Something that the man said triggers a feeling of fear and discomfort.
- His agenda concerning the relationship is much different than is hers.
- He is verbally abusive.
- He breaks or strikes things in anger. He uses symbolic violence (tearing a wedding photo, marring a face in a photo).
- He resolves conflict with intimidation, bullying, and violence.
- He uses threats and intimidation as instruments of control or abuse. This includes threats to harm physically, to defame, to embarrass, to restrict freedom, to disclose secrets, to cut off support, to abandon, and to commit suicide.
- He has battered in previous relationships.
- He uses alcohol or drugs with adverse affects (hostility, loss of memory, cruelty).
- His history includes police encounters for behavioral offenses including stalking, threats, battery, and assault.
- He uses money to control the activities, purchases, and behavior of his wife/partner.
- He becomes jealous of anyone and anything that takes her time away from the relationship; he keeps her on a "tight leash," requires her to account for her time, and wants access to her calendar and planner.
- He discourages her from visiting and having contact with her family and close friends without him.
- He refuses to accept rejection.
- He expects the relationship to go on forever "no matter what."
- He downplays incidents of abuse and assigns fault for the incidents to her.
- He spends a disproportionate amount of time talking about his wife/partner and derives much of his identity from being her husband/lover.
- He has inappropriately surveilled or followed his wife/partner.
- He believes others are out to get him. He believes that his wife's friends encourage her to leave him.
- He resists change and is described as being inflexible.
- He suffers mood swings or is sullen, angry, or depressed.
- He refers to weapons as instruments of power, control, or revenge.

- He consistently blames others for problems of his own making; he refuses to take responsibility for the results of his actions.
- Weapons are a substantial part of his persona.
- He uses "male privilege" as a justification for his conduct. He makes all the major decisions and sees himself as the master of the house.
- He experienced or witnessed violence as a child.
- His wife/partner/girlfriend fears he will injure or kill her. She may have discussed this with others or may have made plans that are to be carried out in the event of her death.

Issues of Suicide

John is an 18-year-old high school senior. He lives at home with his parents, two younger brothers, and a dog. Until eight weeks ago, he was an active, energetic, high-spirited young man. His grades were in the A/B+ column, and he was considered to be an interested and involved student who looked forward to graduation and college life. John and Jenny, his girlfriend since sixth grade, were nearly inseparable. John was quoted as saying that as long as he had "Jenny, football and his Lab retriever, life was great."

Two months ago, Jenny announced her need to back away from her primary relationship with John. Graduation and going away to college would be the "perfect opportunity to move on and grow."

John spent the next two weeks pretending that Jenny would reverse her decision. As reality set in, his behavior reflected the pain and disappointment he felt. All of the joy, the enthusiasm, and the anticipation of graduation dried up. He lacked the energy to bathe, the interest to go to school, and the will to care. His brothers complained that they had to take care of his dog. He kept the curtains in his room closed and the door locked. He ate very little and slept poorly.

John's father declared that this was just a stage that he would pass through soon. His mother cried. They both took comfort in the fact that he was not taking drugs or drinking. His mother finally persuaded him to speak with the school counselor.

When John spoke with the school counselor (SC), she asked him what he was feeling.

JOHN: *I feel restless. It's like I'm looking for something but can't seem to find it.*
SC: *What are you looking for, John?*

JOHN: *Mostly comfort, I guess. Something to stop the hurt.*

SC: *What else?*

JOHN: *I don't want to see anyone; not even friends and family. I guess that's selfish . . .*

SC: *That happens when we don't feel well. I'm interested in listening to you.*

JOHN: *I can't seem to concentrate.*

SC: *Is there anything that holds your attention?*

JOHN: *Whether life is worth living.*

SC: *Do you mean whether your life is worth living?*

JOHN: *Yes, me . . . my life . . .*

SC: *Are you suicidal, John?*

JOHN: *It has crossed my mind. But, no I'm not.*

SC: *Have you ever been suicidal?*

JOHN: *No. I have never had a reason to even consider it before. That's the whole thing here. Can I talk to you about this?*

SC: *Of course! What you have to say is important to me.*

JOHN: *OK. My whole future revolved around having a life with Jenny. I thought we would marry, have kids, buy a house—you know, the whole dream. We would grow old together. I had everything I wanted and I was lead to believe that she did, too. We made these plans in sixth grade and never looked back. Right now, I feel betrayed and angry and used and incredibly sad. It's like somebody cut my guts out of me. If I couldn't trust Jenny, then who and what in life can I trust? Can you understand what I'm experiencing?*

SC: *Yes and I appreciate you trusting me. I know that this is very hurtful. Your feelings are certainly normal given the situation. Is there more that you want to tell me?*

JOHN: *What do I do now?*

SC: *What do you want to do, John?*

JOHN: *I feel some relief. Can I come talk to you again tomorrow?*

SC: *Yes. I want you to agree that you will not do any harm to yourself without speaking to me first. If you agree please read and sign this agreement.*

WHAT TO LOOK FOR

As you intervene, stay alert for what you might observe. Mood swings accompany teen years. Everyone feels sad at times. Feeling sad is not the focus here. A depressed mood that continues for two weeks or more could be a significant sign that deserves attention. Listen to what the teen says and watch what he/she does. Help could be needed if you hear: "I am sleeping much later than I used to"; "I'm not sleeping well and I wake up early in the morning"; or "I am beginning to take a lot of naps" could be cause for some concern. Changes in appetite and unplanned weight gains or losses are additional clues.

LISTEN FOR:

- "I am very restless."
- "I don't want to see anyone; not even friends and family."
- "I can't seem to concentrate anymore."
- "I've lost interest in everything."
- "I feel guilty," or "I feel hopeless or helpless."
- "I seem to be withdrawing more and more."
- "My mood keeps changing."
- "Life is just not worth living anymore."
- "My parents will be really sorry when I'm gone."
- "Bully Billy won't be able to find me where I'm going.

MORE CLUES:

1. It seems to be that young people who have attempted suicide in the past are at greater risk.
2. Talking about suicide does not obviate the need for concern and intervention. Those who talk about suicide might actually do it. It is a myth to think otherwise.
3. Feelings of loneliness, hopelessness, and rejection are significant.
4. Alcohol use and abuse might be a part of suicidal behavior. Some teens who use or abuse alcohol or drugs are more likely to consider, attempt, or succeed at suicide than are non-abusers.
5. Those planning to kill themselves might give away personal possessions, discard things that are usually meaningful to them, or begin cleaning their own room.
6. The teen may suddenly become cheerful, or even appear upbeat, after a bout with depression. The change might foretell that they have made the decision to end their own life. Do not put off getting help in those circumstances.
7. One of the most dangerous times occurs when severe loss of any kind has been experienced or personal humiliation has been felt.

PROCEDURES FOR RESPONDING TO A SUICIDAL PERSON

1. Act early. If you suspect suicide, take action now. Make contact early. Do not leave the sufferer alone.
2. Speak of suicide openly. If you can talk openly about it, maybe it will be easier for the sufferer to open up. Using the word *suicide* will not make the person suicidal. Tell the sufferer, "I don't want you to die." Listen carefully to what is said. Reassure and remain calm. Let the sufferer talk and let him/her know that you are trying to understand his/her hurt.
3. Never say, "You don't really want to do that." The sufferer really does want to do it.
4. Never ask, "Why do you want to do that?" The sufferer probably doesn't know "why," and the question will increase his/her defensiveness. Ask present-oriented questions if you need information: "What happened?"; "How do you feel?"; "What's going on?"; "Would you like to talk about it?"
5. A suicidal person will have trouble focusing on the future and that, "Things will get better." Keep your focus on the present and what can be done to assist the sufferer now.
6. Never challenge the sufferer to "Go ahead and do it." You may be giving him/her permission to do the act.
7. Carefully select anyone you plan to contact. That person may be part of the problem (e.g., family members, minister, doctor). The best person to handle a suicidal individual is a trained police negotiator.
8. Remember that suicide has nothing to do with death. Suicide has to do with conflict in a person's life between the sufferer and at least one other person or institution, either present or absent, in the person's life at the moment.
9. If you believe that the person is suicidal, do not leave him/her alone. If physically with the person, stay with him/her or get someone else to stay if you have to leave. If on the phone, stay on the phone to the degree that you can. If you must get off the phone, or if the sufferer gets off, make contact again without unnecessary delay.
10. Check out the "specificity of the suicidal plan" and the "lethality of the suicidal means." The more specific the plan and the more lethal the means, the greater the risk of suicide. Ask the sufferer what he/she intends to do and how. You should have a plan in place to cover several possibilities.

Intervener Survival

High stress levels, personal frustration, and inadequate coping skills have major personal, organizational, and social costs. Stress is not a mental illness, but a part of everyday living. Each of us is potentially vulnerable to the problems of too much stress and too little coping ability.

Signs and Symptoms of Stress and Burnout

1. High resistance to going to work every day.
2. A pervasive sense of failure, as indicated by such expressions as "I can't do enough"; "I can't get it right"; "I'm no good anymore."
3. Anger and resentment.
4. Guilt and blame. These might be expressed by such expressions as, "No matter how many hours I work, I never finish and I feel guilty about leaving. I'm in a 'no-win' situation."
5. Discouragement and indifference.
6. Negativism.
7. Isolation and withdrawal.
8. Feelings of tiredness and exhaustion.
9. Frequent clock watching.
10. Extreme fatigue after work.
11. Loss of positive feelings.
12. Postponement of victim contacts.
13. Inability to concentrate or listen to information.
14. Feelings of immobilization.
15. Cynicism toward victims, co-workers, or the world in general.
16. Sleep disorders, including difficulty either in falling asleep or in staying asleep, or sleeping an adequate amount but not

feeling rested upon waking. These disorders occur regularly over an extended period.

17. Self-preoccupation.
18. Becoming more approving of behavior-control measures, such as tranquilizers.
19. Frequent colds and flus.
20. Frequent headaches and gastrointestinal disturbances.
21. Rigidity in thinking and resistance to change.
22. Suspicion and paranoia.
23. Excessive drug use.
24. Marital and family conflict.
25. Free-floating anxiety, evidenced by such expressions as, "I am constantly worried and anxious, but I can't pinpoint what I'm upset about. It just seems to hover there."
26. Tunnel vision: as stress increases, perception of available options narrows.
27. A sense of increasing helplessness.
28. Fear that "it won't get better."
29. Fear of losing control.
30. High absenteeism.

Intervener and victim alike are subject to stressors, and both can become incapacitated as a result of unmanaged stress.

The authors began addressing issues of intervener survival in late 1970. We recognized that a person in crisis cannot provide effective assistance to another person who is also in crisis. Therefore, it seemed a logical step to incorporate into our Crisis Intervention training and into our writing an ongoing discussion on the importance of self-awareness, self-protection, proper nutrition, time to play, personal stress management, and wellness as one prepares to be an intervener. The discussion continues to be about humor and balance, preparation, and seeking clarity in one's professional and personal life. It is about taking responsibility for being a responsible intervener.

Teachable Moments in Crisis Intervention

As explained in Chapter 1 of this book, the basic role of the intervener is to effectively diffuse a potentially disastrous situation and to help the sufferer to return to his or her level of pre-crisis functioning. Be alert to the potential for teachable moments. These possibilities can occur during the assessment, the disposition, and the referral. No lectures. No biased propaganda. Use personal opinions sparingly, if at all. Personal opinions should be labeled as such. Use well-placed questions to draw out the sufferer's own ideas and options for managing the problem. Use appropriate encouragers, model active listening, provide accurate information, recognize the moment when a "light bulb" seems to come on. That is a teachable moment. Taking care of oneself does not guarantee effective Crisis Intervention; it enhances the possibility of a success intervention.

Keep Stress Within Tolerable Limits

The following are suggestions for keeping stress within tolerable limits:

1. Eliminate stressor foods from your diet. Nutritional stress can be as debilitating as emotional stress.
2. Get enough sleep and rest.
3. Exercise regularly and appropriately for your age and fitness level.
4. Be realistic about the givens of your world. Work within the reality of "what is" today.
5. Realistically assess what you are able to do in your particular situation.
6. Schedule time for fun. Allow time each day to experience good feelings.
7. Schedule time each week for dreaming, thinking, wandering, exploring, planning, and being in touch with your dreams.
8. Schedule regular recreation or vacation time. The quantity of time spent is not important; the quality of time spent in recreation is a key to stress reduction.
9. Be sure you receive your minimum daily requirement of positive nurturing.
10. Set realistic goals in all areas of your life.
11. Consider the following carefully:
    a. Everything I do is the result of a choice I make.
    b. Every choice I make benefits me positively in some way even though I may not know what the benefit is at the moment.
    c. I have inside me everything I need and all the tools I need to guide my life successfully.

    d. I can choose to gain greater self-awareness.

    e. I am responsible for 100 percent of my life.

    f. The degree to which others control my life is the degree to which I allow them to control it.

    g. I cannot voluntarily change my feelings, but I can always change my behavior.

    h. Any problem I experience in my life is a problem that I have created for myself.

    i. If I choose to continue creating a particular problem for myself, I do it because

        (1) I receive some pleasure or unacknowledged benefit or payoff for continuing the problem, or

        (2) I can avoid a greater or more fearful problem by perpetuating the current problem. In other words, if I solve the current problem, I am afraid the greater problem will occur.

12. Develop interests outside of your specialized field.

13. Identify what is important to you.

14. Find someone to talk to.

15. Surround yourself with people who have a positive attitude.

16. Find an ongoing support system to access as needed.

17. Be aware of situations that may trigger an unresolved issue.

18. Recognize the effect that the sufferer's pain has on you.

19. Acknowledge the feelings that you have and allow them to be whatever they are.

20. Recognize that working harder, faster, longer, or punishing your body will not relieve the pain.

21. Recognize that neglecting your own needs, interests, or health will eventually create more pain.

22. Slot into your appointment book a time for yourself. This does not require a lengthy period of time. It does needs to be do-able. Be creative.

Preventing Organizational Burnout

There is often a direct relationship between burnout in a workplace and a pervasive unwillingness to deal with the givens or realities of a situation. When unrealistically high expectations infiltrate the culture of a workplace and high stress levels become commonplace, the agency begins to show signs of organizational burnout: high absenteeism, lack of teamwork, tension among staff workers, decreased productivity, and, ultimately, high turnover. A group of disgruntled staff workers remain because they can't afford to leave yet. This should concern managers or supervisors of agencies, health care settings, corporations, schools, and virtually all other workplace settings. The director's expectations might not fit with what is feasible. Caseloads might be overburdening. Staff might be limited in size and training. The director might be asked to handle situations that the agency is not equipped to handle. These concerns, coupled with a lack of funds and the overabundance of paperwork, might be some of the problems that the director of an agency faces on a daily basis.

The following discussion is written for directors and supervisors. The importance of being able to assess realistically what you are able to do within the framework of a situation is essential to stress reduction. Problems of budget constraints, limited staff, overflowing paperwork, faxes, e-mails, text messages, phone calls, and large caseloads were mentioned in the previous paragraph. Given the situation, how will you allocate the budget that you do have? How will you administer the program with the existing staff? How can you work best within the existing facilities? What can you do to maintain a high level of staff morale? How can you foster an atmosphere conducive to productivity? In short, what can you and your staff do to minimize unwanted stress?

Will you spend your time as director being frustrated, wishing for a miracle that doesn't come, thereby creating additional anxiety within yourself and your staff? Or are you willing to use your energy to direct your agency along positive lines? How will you choose to arrange your life within the framework of what currently exists for you, your task, and those with whom you work at the moment? It is a very important choice that impacts your health and the health of your facility. The choice represents an opportunity to deal with stress management in your own life. It is also interesting to note the paradox that might be operating in these situations. The degree to which you exercise your choice to reduce stress in your life is the same degree to which some of your hopes for the future may be more nearly attainable.

The following suggestions are directed to managers and supervisors. The list is not intended to be exhaustive. We present this universal formula with the hope that you will tailor it to your particular environment. Let this be a catalyst for planning creatively, exploring options, and being innovative. Enjoy the process and the results.

DR. LEVITON'S 50 STEPS TO PROACTIVE MANAGEMENT FOR
REDUCING STRESS IN THE WORKPLACE

1. Be clear in preparing a job description.
2. Be clear in the interview with the perspective staff member.
3. Be clear in delegating responsibility.
4. Be clear in assigning tasks.
5. Be realistic in assigning responsibilities.
6. Be realistic in expectations of self and staff.
7. See the big picture. Every decision has an impact and a consequence. Nothing operates in a vacuum.
8. Respond. Don't react. This principle should be observed up and down the chain of employees.
9. Plan and then act.
10. Be consistent. Don't keep changing the rules. When employees are unclear about policy and function, their level of stress and anxiety escalates. Feeling out of structure without a mechanism for relief potentially results in crisis.
11. Be reliable. Act reliably. Ensure that your actions match your words.
12. Create an environment that is orderly and efficient.
13. Be explicit in setting policy. Apply the policy in an even-handed manner.
14. Provide support, structure, and information to your staff.
15. Encourage and place a value on staff creativity and innovation.
16. Communicate in a timely, appropriate, accurate manner.
17. Be accessible. When and how can you be reached?
18. Meet your employees and call them by name if at all possible. If you tell them you care, then show it. To be trusted, you must be honest.
19. Take field trips through your facility.
20. Be aware of your surroundings. You will gain valuable information about how things are going by using your sensing mechanisms.
21. Encourage input from your staff. It is all right not to have all the answers. Involving staff members increases their job satisfaction, commitment, and dedication to both the company and the job.
22. Give directions as needed and as appropriate.

23. Give feedback on a timely schedule.
24. Be fair. Act fairly despite personal biases.
25. Encourage professional development.
26. Create a safe environment. This includes both physical and emotional safety. Be clear that harassment of any nature will not be tolerated. Take necessary actions immediately if violations of the policy occur.
27. Create a supportive and non-defensive climate.
28. Identify potential stressors in your work environment.
29. Recognize symptoms of stress in yourself and in your staff.
30. Be aware of the relationship of unmanaged stress and crisis.
31. Understand the relationship of stress/crisis/burnout.
32. Decide how to respond to the stress that you are experiencing, the signs of stress that the staff member is exhibiting, and the potential stressors that you observed. Use what you have learned from earlier chapters in this book.
33. Recognize the cost of burnout to your agency.
34. Recognize the benefit to your organization of effective intervention.
35. Accept personal responsibility for your feelings and your behavior.
36. Allow your feelings to be what they are.
37. Separate your feelings from your behavior. You cannot always voluntarily change your feelings, but you can always voluntarily change your actions.
38. Be realistic about the givens of your world.
39. Realistically assess what you can do in your particular situation.
40. Set realistic goals in all areas of your life.
41. Get sufficient rest and sleep.
42. Eliminate stressor foods from your diet. Nutritional stress can be as debilitating as emotional stress.
43. Schedule time on your calendar for fun. Allow time each day to experience good feelings.
44. Schedule time each week on your calendar for dreaming, thinking, wandering, exploring, and planning. Quiet time has special benefits.
45. Encourage peer networks of support among employees.
46. Teach conflict resolution skills to your staff.

47. Recognize that evaluation of employee performance should be a continuous process rather than an occasional event.
    a. Discuss the evaluation procedure in advance with the supervisee.
    b. Encourage the supervisee to do a self-evaluation.
    c. Keep the focus of the evaluation on the supervisee's work performance.
    d. Review strengths and weaknesses, growth and stagnation. Be fair and clear.
    e. Focus on modifiable aspects of the supervisee's performance.
    f. Formulate the evaluations with some consistency. Apply the same standards in the same way to all of the supervisees who have approximately the same education and experience.
48. Recognize the necessity of humor in the workplace.
49. Be aware that you set the climate for your organization.
50. Remember that most employees would like to feel a sense of commitment, challenge, and some control in their assignments.

Reactions of Children to Crisis

The adult members of the family came home after the funeral. Judy, aged six, ran to her mother and hugged her. Judy asked a few questions about the funeral ceremony but as usual got no satisfying answers. Her mother tearfully replied, "Grandma is in heaven now. Go see if Amy can play with you this afternoon."

Judy had had a special relationship with her grandmother. Mrs. Brown lived with the Smiths until she required institutional care. Judy never really understood why her grandmother had been sent away. In fact, there were a lot of things Judy wondered and worried about. Why couldn't she visit her grandmother after she became ill? What did Grandma look like when she was sick? How would she find out the end of the stories Grandma told her? How will she be able to share secrets with Grandma now? Her biggest concern was what did she do bad to make Grandma leave her? Now that Grandma's gone to heaven, who will answer her questions?

Judy didn't want to play. She was afraid to disturb her mother. She felt lonely, stuck, and desperately in need of talking with Grandma.

Childhood crisis might be more difficult to assess than adult crisis. Children have a limited fund of experience with which to handle crisis, limited cognitive structure, limited training, and usually an immature emotional base. Perhaps even more important is the fact that very young children have not yet developed a sense of cause and effect or a sense of time. Therefore, whatever pain occurs seems to go on forever. As the child becomes older and struggles with his/her identity, independence, psychological changes, peer pressures, and cultural and parental demands, the potential for heightened stress increases. Often, as occurred with Judy, the child's need for help goes unrecognized, ignored, or belittled. Often, as occurred with Judy, the child is told to go out and play; to be a big boy or a big girl; to be the man of the house now that Daddy is gone as a result of divorce, military service, job transfer, or illness; or to be seen but not heard.

Often, in an act of protectiveness, parents exclude children from discussions of crises. Questions may be answered evasively or not at all, as in the case of Judy. Protectiveness carried to extremes may result in the child's having little ability to communicate concerns, to have questions answered, or to establish the cognitive and emotional channels necessary for his/her own adaptation to change and loss.

The intervener can help the child deal with concerns such as:

- Threat to nurturance
- Changing patterns of expression of feelings
- Disrupted patterns of communication
- Changes in lifestyle because of finances
- Disrupted scheduling
- Necessity of assuming responsibilities beyond his/her abilities
- Perception of loss
- The need to grieve

Difficulties with schoolwork and peer relationships; excessive withdrawal; repeated angry outbursts; and involvement in repetitive, ritualistic, symbolic acts may reflect the stresses experienced by the child. These difficulties can be managed through skillful intervention.

As an example, in intervening with Judy, the little girl in the case described above, the following procedure might have been used by her mother:

1. Legitimize her feelings. Judy clearly expressed her need to be heard and her frustration at being discounted. She felt abandoned by her grandmother, yet possibly responsible for her leaving them through some unknown behavior on her part. She grieved over unfinished business with her grandmother. There was no chance to hear the end of the stories and share secrets. An effective intervener would listen to the child and acknowledge her feelings with honesty and caring.
2. Provide Judy information according to her emotional and cognitive capacity. Perhaps the mother could explain: "Grandma did not desert you; and we did not send her away. Sometimes

people need care that they can best get in a hospital or a special nursing home. Mommy and Daddy loved Grandma as you do, and we wanted her to have the best care possible. We picked a very special place that we thought she would like. Grandma loved you very much. She enjoyed telling you those stories. Soon you will be able to read them yourself. That might be a special way of spending some pretend time with Grandma."

3. Assure her that Grandma is no longer suffering pain or discomfort. "I saw Grandma after she died. She looked comfortable and not in pain." It is not necessary at this time to go into a long, detailed description. Judy merely needs some reassurance about what dead people and her grandmother in particular look like.

4. Offer to take Judy to the gravesite. Allow it to be her choice to accept or reject the offer. Going there will provide her with an opportunity for visiting with Grandma and seeing the site. Let her dictate whether she wants you to stand beside her or would prefer a few moments of privacy with her grandmother. Afterward, ask if she has any other questions or wants to share any ideas or feelings. Judy might just jump in the car and suggest getting an ice-cream cone. The relief of seeing that everything is in order is an important part of the adaptation process.

5. Provide her the nurturing that she asked for. Return her hug and hold her. Let her know by your touch that you are not pushing her away.

6. If necessary, explain that you are tired now and would like some time alone. At this point, Judy can probably accept your need to move to some other activity. Her immediate needs have been met.

General Reactions of Children to Crisis

Although many feelings and reactions are shared by people of all ages in response to the direct or indirect effects of crisis, meeting the needs of children requires special attention.

Typical reactions of children, regardless of age, include the following:

- Fears stemming from the crisis extending to their home or neighborhood
- Loss of interest in school
- Regressive behavior
- Sleep disturbances and night terrors
- Fears of events that may be associated with the crisis situation, such as airplane sounds or loud noises

Reactions of Specific Age Groups

Children of different age groups tend to react in unique ways to the stress caused by crises and their consequences. The following typical reactions to stress are summarized for each age group and are followed by suggested responses.

Preschool (Ages 1–5)

Typical reactions to stress include the following:

- Thumb-sucking
- Bed-wetting
- Fear of the dark or of animals
- Clinging to parents
- Night terrors
- Loss of bladder or bowel control or constipation
- Speech difficulties
- Loss of or increase in appetite
- Fear of being left alone
- Immobility

Children in this age group are particularly vulnerable to disruption of their previously secure world. Because they lack the verbal and conceptual skills necessary to cope effectively with sudden stress by themselves, they look to family members for comfort. These children are often strongly affected by the reactions of parents and other family members.

Abandonment is a major fear in this age group. Children who have lost family members (or even pets or toys) because of circumstances either related or unrelated to the crisis will need special reassurance.

We recommend the following responses to help children integrate their experiences and reestablish a sense of security and mastery:

- Encourage expression through play reenactment where appropriate.
- Provide verbal reassurance and physical comforting.
- Give the child frequent attention.
- Encourage the child's expression of feelings and concerns regarding the loss, temporary or permanent, of family members, pets, toys, or friends.
- Provide comforting bedtime routines.
- Allow the child to sleep in the same room with the parent. Make it clear to the child that this is only for a limited period.

Early Childhood (Ages 5–11)

Common reactions to stress in this age group include the following:

- Irritability
- Whining
- Clinging
- Aggressive behavior at home or at school
- Overt competition with younger siblings for parent's attention
- Night terrors, nightmares, or fear of darkness
- School avoidance
- Loss of interest and poor concentration in school
- Fear of personal harm
- Confusion
- Fear of abandonment
- Generalized anxiety

Fear of loss is particularly difficult for these children to handle, and regressive behavior is most typical of this age group.

We recommend the following responses:

- Patience and tolerance
- Play sessions with adults and peers where affective reactions can be openly discussed

- Discussions with adults and peers about frightening anxiety-producing aspects of events and about appropriate behavior to manage the child's concerns and the stress
- Relaxation of expectations at school or at home (It should be made clear to the child that this relaxation is temporary and that the normal routine will be resumed after a suitable period.)
- Opportunities for structured, but not unusually demanding, chores and responsibilities at home
- Maintenance of a familiar routine as much as possible and as soon as possible

Preadolescent (Ages 11–14)

The following are common reactions to stress for this age group:

- Sleep disturbances
- Appetite disturbance
- Rebellion in the home
- Refusal to do chores
- School problems, such as fighting, withdrawal, loss of interest, and attention-seeking behavior
- Physical problems, such as headaches, vague aches and pains, skin eruptions, bowel problems, and psychosomatic complaints
- Loss of interest in peer social activities
- Fear of personal harm; fear of impending loss of family members, friends, or home
- Anger
- Denial
- Generalized anxiety

Peer reactions are especially significant in preadolescence. These children need to feel that their fears are both appropriate and shared by others. Responses should be aimed at assessing tensions, anxieties, and possible guilt feelings.

We recommend the following responses:

- Group activities geared toward the resumption of routines
- Involvement with same age group activity
- Group discussions geared toward examining feelings about the crisis and appropriate behavior to manage the concerns and the stress
- Structured, but undemanding, responsibilities

- Temporarily relaxed expectations of performance at school and at home
- Additional individual attention and consideration

Adolescent (Ages 14–18)

Common reactions in this age group include the following:

- Psychosomatic symptoms, such as rashes, bowel problems, and asthma
- Headaches and tension
- Appetite and sleep disturbances
- Hypochondriasis
- Amenorhhea or dysmenorrhea
- Agitation or decrease in energy level
- Apathy
- Decline in interest in the opposite sex
- Irresponsible behavior, delinquent behavior, or both
- Decline in emancipatory struggles over parental control
- Poor concentration
- Guilt
- Fear of loss
- Anger at the perceived unfairness of a crisis occurring in their lives
- Tendency to blame others for negative events that befall them

Most of the activities and interests of adolescents are focused in their own age-group peers. Adolescents tend to be especially distressed by the disruption of their peer-group activities and by their lack of access to full adult responsibilities in community efforts.

We recommend the following responses:

- Encourage participation in the community and in individual responses such as letter writing.
- Encourage discussion of feelings, concerns, and shared information with peers and extra-family significant others.
- Temporarily reduce expectations for specific levels of both school and general performance, depending on individual reactions.
- Encourage, but do not insist on, discussions of crisis-induced fears within the family setting.

When to Refer Children to Mental Health Professionals

A wide range of normal reactions surround crisis. Usually the reactions can be dealt with by support at home and at school, but this is not always the case. Sometimes a teacher needs to recommend professional help. In making such a referral, it is important to stress that it is not a sign of the parents' failure if they find that they cannot help their child by themselves. It is also important to note that early action will help the child return to normal functioning and avoid more severe problems later.

Students who have lost family members or friends, either temporarily or permanently, or feel that they were in extreme danger are at special risk. Those who have been involved in individual or family crises in addition to the crisis they are currently experiencing might have more difficulty dealing with the additional stress. Counseling may be recommended as a preventive measure when these circumstances are known to exist.

Referral is recommended when symptoms that are considered normal reactions persist for several months or disrupt the student's social, mental, or physical functioning.

Referral for Preschool and Elementary School Children

Consider referring the family for professional help if the children react in these ways:

- Seem excessively withdrawn
- Do not respond to special attention and attempts to draw them out

Referral for Junior and Senior High School Children

Consider referral to a mental health professional if students react in the following ways:

- Are disoriented; for example, are unable to give their own name and address or the date
- Complain of significant memory gaps
- Are despondent and show agitation, restlessness, and pacing
- Are severely depressed and withdrawn
- Mutilate themselves
- Use drugs or alcohol excessively

- Are unable to care for themselves in such areas as eating, drinking, bathing, and dressing
- Repeat ritualistic acts
- Experience hallucinations, such as hearing voices or seeing visions
- State that their body feels "unreal" and express the concern that they are "going crazy"
- Are excessively preoccupied with one idea or thought
- Have the delusion that someone or something is out to get them and their family
- Are afraid that they will commit suicide or kill another person
- Are unable to make simple decisions or carry out everyday functions
- Show extremely pressured speech or talk overflow
- Exhibit chronic disruptive behavior
- Make self-destructive decisions

Classroom Activities

Creative classroom activities help teachers seeking ways to deal with the stress and tension a crisis and its consequences create in students. The following activities are vehicles for expression and discussion for students and are important steps in helping children handle the stress they are experiencing. You can use these activities to stimulate your own ideas and adapt them to meet both your students' needs and your teaching style.

Preschool Activities

1. Make available some toys that encourage play enactment of the child's concerns. Such toys might include airplanes, helicopters, toy police officers, toy soldiers, rescue trucks, ambulances, building blocks, puppets, or dolls. Playing with these toys allows the child to ventilate feelings about what is occurring or has already occurred.
2. Children need a lot of physical contact during times of stress to help them reestablish ego boundaries and a sense of security. Introduce games that involve physical toughening among

children within a structure. Examples include "Ring Around the Rosy," "London Bridge," and "Duck, Duck, Goose."

3. Provide extra amounts of drinks and finger foods in small portions. This is a concrete way of supplying the emotional and physical nourishment children need in times of stress. Oral satisfaction is especially necessary because children tend to revert to more regressive behavior in response to feeling that their survival or security is threatened.

4. Have the children make a mural on butcher paper, using topics related to what is happening in the world and in their community. This is recommended for small groups, with discussion afterward facilitated by the teacher or other skilled adult.

5. Have the children draw individual pictures about the crisis situation and then discuss the pictures in small groups. This activity allows children to vent their experiences and to discover that others share their fears.

6. Make a group collage, and discuss what the collage represents, how it was made, and the feelings it evokes.

Elementary School Activities

1. For younger children, make toys available that encourage play to express concerns, fears, and observations. These toys might include ambulances, planes, tanks, helicopters, toy police officers, rescue vehicles, fire trucks, building blocks, and dolls. Play with puppets can provide ways for older children, as well as younger children, to ventilate their feelings.

2. Help or encourage the children to develop skits or puppet shows about what happened during the crisis. Encourage them to include anything positive about the experience as well as frightening or disconcerting aspects.

3. Have the children create short stories about the crisis and how it was managed. These stories can be either written or dictated to an adult, depending on the age of the child.

4. Have the children draw pictures and discuss them in relation to the crisis. It is important that the group discussion end on a positive note if at all possible. Mastery and having a vehicle for expressing concerns are equally important.

5. Stimulate group discussion about crisis and its consequences by showing your own feelings and fears. It is very important to legitimize children's fears and to help children feel less isolated. It is equally important to give them a sense of structure, balance, and control over their own activities and life.

6. Have the children brainstorm their own ways of handling their concerns. Encourage them to discuss the results with their parents.

7. Encourage class activities in which the children can organize and build projects such as scrapbooks to give them a sense of mastery and ability to organize what seems chaotic and confusing.

8. Encourage the children to talk about their own feelings about the crisis.

9. Have children brainstorm ways to be supportive of the family after the death of a classmate or a family's loss of a home because of a natural disaster. Have the students take steps to follow up on their plan.

Junior and Senior High School Activities

1. Conduct a group discussion of the students' experiences concerning the crisis situation and the events surrounding it. This is particularly important to adolescents because they need the opportunity to vent as well as to normalize the extreme emotions that arise in them. A good way to stimulate such a discussion is for you to share your personal reactions. The students might need considerable reassurance that even extreme emotions and "crazy" thoughts are normal under these circumstances. It is important to end such discussions on a positive note. Such discussion is appropriate for any course of study because it can hasten a return to more normal functioning.

2. Conduct a class discussion or support a class project on how students might involve themselves in activities related to managing the crisis. This might include support groups, rallies, and assistance to family members. It is important to help students develop concrete, realistic ways to assist or to be involved. This helps them to overcome the feelings of helplessness, frustration, and guilt common to these situations.

3. Introduce classroom activities that relate the crisis and its consequences to course study. This can be an effective way to help students integrate their own experiences or observations while providing specific learning experiences. In performing these activities, it is important to allow time for the students to discuss feelings stimulated by the projects or the issues covered.

The following suggestions could be carried on within specific courses. Teachers are encouraged to expand these suggestions to fit the students' needs and the teacher's individual style.

Journalism Have the students write stories that cover different aspects of the crisis. These might include stories about community and personal impact, human interest, and ecological impact. You might also discuss issues such as accurate reporting, censorship, sensationalism, and students could compile the stories into a special publication.

Science Discuss the scientific aspects of the crisis, such as weapons and their destructive power, research, impact of the weather, environmental impact, and impact on the school. Suggest a project about stress involving the physiological responses to stress and methods of dealing with it.

English Composition Have the students write about their own experiences, or those of persons close to them, regarding the crisis and the problems associated with it. You might discuss composition issues, such as the problems that arise in conveying heavy emotional tone without being overly dramatic.

Literature Have students report on crises that have occurred in mythology or that appear in fiction and poetry.

Psychology Have the students apply what they have learned in the course to the emotions, behaviors, and stress reactions they felt or observed in response to the crisis. Cover post traumatic stress syndrome as appropriate. Present a guest speaker from the mental health profession who may be working with families affected by the crisis or with support groups. Have students discuss from their own experience what has helped them most in dealing with crisis-related stress. Have the students develop a mental health education brochure in which they discuss emotional and behavioral reactions to crisis and the things that are helpful in coping.

Peer Counseling Provide special information about common responses to the onset of the crisis and the consequences associated with it. Encourage the students to help each other integrate their own experiences.

Health Discuss emotional reactions to crisis and the importance of taking care of one's own emotional and physical well-being. Discuss health implications of crisis including food, water, physical, and mental wounds, exposure to the elements, and other health precautions and safety measures. Discuss the effects of adrenalin on the body during stress and danger. A public health or mental health professional could be invited to speak to the class. Maintaining health, from the viewpoints of all those involved in or affected by the crisis, might be a very valuable discussion topic.

Art Have the students portray the crisis and their concerns about it in various art media. Students can do this individually or in a group.

Speech and Drama Have the students portray the emotions, feelings, and stresses that have arisen in response to the crisis and the effects of the crisis on each of them. Ask students to develop a skit or play on some aspect of the crisis.

Math Have the class solve mathematical problems related to the impact of the crisis.

Civics and Government Study governmental agencies responsible either directly or indirectly for causing or supporting the crisis and their response to the crisis. Discuss how these agencies work and the impact of each agency. Examine various community systems and how the stress of the crisis has affected them. Have the students invite a local government official to class to discuss how the crisis has affected the community.

History Have the students report on crises that have occurred both around the world and in the geographical location of the current crisis.

AGE-SPECIFIC REACTIONS OF CHILDREN AFFECTED BY CRISIS AND ITS CONSEQUENCES

Preschoolers	Elementary School Children	Preadolescents/ Adolescents
Crying	Headaches/physical complaints	Headaches/physical complaints
Thumb-sucking	Depression	Depression
Loss of bowel control	Fears about safety	Confusion
Fears of being left alone and of strangers	Confusion	Poor performance
Irritability	Inability to concentrate	Aggressive behavior
Confusion	Poor performance	Withdrawal
Clinging	Fighting	Isolation
Immobility	Withdrawal from peers	

AGE-SPECIFIC INTERVENTIONS FOR CHILDREN REACTING TO CRISIS

Preschoolers	Elementary School Children	Preadolescents/ Adolescents
Draw a picture	Draw a picture	Stories and essays
Tell a story	Tell a story	Books on effects of crisis
Coloring books	Books on effects of crisis	Create a play about the crisis
Books on effects of crisis	Create a game	School project/ natural sciences
Doll, toy play	Create a play	School project/ social sciences
Group games	School study project	School health project
Talks about safety	Materials about personal and family safety	Materials about personal and family safety and community protection

What lessons can and have been learned that could benefit us and our communities in the future?

Other chapters in this book include additional examples of children's reactions to crisis events. Regardless of the particular event, the basic intervention procedure will apply.

Hot-Line Workers

The immediacy of crisis situations dictates the need for immediate service delivery. Hot-line services are as close as the telephone and are usually available 24 hours a day, seven days a week. As a rule, the caller can obtain assistance without the need for self-identification.

Hot-line work is difficult. It requires that the intervener compensate for the inability to see the caller's appearance, behavior, and body language as the caller speaks or listens. The intervener must remain focused and free of distractions that could impede his or her ability to listen to the caller. We recommend the following "do's" and "don'ts" for hot-line workers.

Do's

DO establish a feeling of trust, support, and confidence.

DO allow the caller to speak freely and to ventilate feelings.

DO listen carefully, not only to what is being said but also to what is not being said.

DO encourage callers to tell you what is troubling them.

DO accept callers' right to feel as they do. The way they see the world at this time in their life is real for them.

DO listen attentively and reflect feelings.

DO be honest. If you do not know an answer or cannot provide the information requested, say so.

DO ask for feedback to find out if you are on the right track.

DO be realistic.

DO ask what the caller is doing currently to manage the particular discomfort the caller is experiencing.

DO ask how the caller has managed traumatic events in the past.

DO help the caller draw from past successes in managing current personal crises.

DO be alert for opportunities to reinforce the caller's strengths and positive qualities.

DO build a sense of structure that the caller can relate to.

DO help callers identify areas in their personal life over which they can assert control. Stress the need to devote energy to these areas rather than to areas over which they have no control.

DO have updated, immediately available referral resources.

DO get in touch and stay in touch with yourself and what you, as the hot-line worker, are feeling.

DO separate your needs, concerns, and values from the caller's. Respond to what the caller needs.

DO debrief with a fellow hot-line worker as needed.

DO trust yourself to ask effective questions, to offer appropriate options, and to know when to stop.

DO remember that your job is to listen, empathize, and help set some sense of structure for the caller, who might feel out of control.

DO remember that hot-line work is stressful. Take time to care for yourself as you care for others.

DO maintain boundaries. Avoid using the situation to resolve a similar or current crisis in your own life.

Don'ts

DON'T offer any service you cannot provide.

DON'T agree or disagree with callers. The way they see the world at this time is real to them.

DON'T interrupt callers while they are talking unless absolutely necessary. If you need more details, wait until the caller is finished, and then go back and ask for the needed information.

DON'T argue with a caller.

DON'T be afraid of silence. Give the caller time to think and feel.

DON'T assume anything. Ask for clarification if you are concerned about the caller's physical and emotional safety.

DON'T allow the caller's anger or hostility to intimidate you.

DON'T push your value system on the caller.

DON'T push your religious beliefs on the caller.

DON'T be afraid to admit that a caller might need further help that you cannot provide. Refer as necessary and as appropriate.

DON'T allow callers to concentrate only on the negative aspects of their situation. Help them develop options.

DON'T show excessive pity or sympathy.

DON'T use the situation for a catharsis about a similar or parallel loss or crisis in your own life. Maintain boundaries.

Twenty Steps for Handling the Difficult Caller

As hot-line workers and phone counselors, our job is to assist, to answer, perhaps to counsel, and certainly to help those who call. Occasionally the caller is upset to the point of belligerency either because of the emotional trauma suffered or because of extreme anger experienced for some other reason. Callers in this situation could become abusive to the hot-line worker and, if not checked appropriately, will contaminate all attempts to be helpful.

The following are suggested as a nonexhaustive guide to handling difficult and abusive calls and callers.

1. Stop talking.
2. Take a deep breath.
3. Listen for the caller's real message.
4. If possible, legitimize the caller's anger.
5. Listen carefully for clues as to what is really going on with the caller.
6. Reduce the volume of your own voice when speaking. Your action might cause the callers to lower their voices also, or at least to stop talking so they can hear what you are saying.
7. Do not argue with the caller or become defensive. The caller's remarks or abuse is usually not intended for you personally. The caller would probably make the same remarks to whoever answered the phone.
8. Clarify your role with the caller.
9. Refuse to be verbally abused by the caller: "I want to listen to what you are saying, but I won't listen to insults, threats, or personal attacks on me."

10. State the ground rules for your being able to provide assistance to the caller. These include the caller's refraining from abusive talk.
11. Keep your responses clear and simple.
12. Once you have stated the ground rules, let the caller decide whether or not he or she wishes to continue the conversation. Continue with the conversation only if the caller agrees to abide by the ground rules.
13. Avoid being judgmental of anything the caller says. Remember, the way the caller sees the world is accurate for that caller.
14. Remember: Do not take personally any abusive remarks the caller makes to you.
15. Ask for and obtain a clear commitment from the caller that he or she will continue the conversation without abusive talk and according to the agreed-upon ground rules.
16. Continue to repeat your willingness to keep trying to assist the caller, and repeat the ground rules for continuing.
17. Always be aware of, and continue to evaluate, the caller's actual threat potential to you.
18. If all else fails in your attempt to deal with the caller's abusive or otherwise difficult behavior, terminate the call.
19. Debrief immediately after a difficult or abusive phone call.
20. Remember: You are the professional and you are in control.

Family Crisis

Excessive stress and tension, usually resulting from multiple or major changes in a person's life, are often the basis of most crisis situations. Because family members do not operate in a vacuum, one person's crisis often becomes a crisis for the family. Major sources of personal crises include illness, financial problems, business problems, job promotions/demotions/or loss, problems with one's children, layoffs, maintenance of a current career or entrance into a new one, adoption or birth of children, abortion, pending marriage, separation and divorce, blending of stepfamilies, severe injuries, deaths in the family, health care issues, eldercare issues, gender issues, safety and protection issues, housing issues, education issues, intimacy and relationship issues.

Most crises have a primary victim, but they also touch those who are affected through the primary victim. These secondary victims are usually significant others of the person experiencing the crisis. In rapes, suicide, battering, incest, drug abuse, family disputes, natural disasters, war, death, and illness, the intensity of the trauma, the emotional upheaval, and the difficulty in adjustment relating to the event can be as severe for the significant others as for the primary victim. Secondary victims often experience their own crisis as they try to fit what has happened into life as they see it. For example, a rape victim's parents, spouse, or boyfriend, or the children who witnessed the rape might experience their own crisis with an intensity equal to that of the primary victim. Guidelines and procedures for crisis situations with primary victims must be applied in a similar manner to significant others. Unfortunately, the intervener often overlooks this task particularly where children are involved. As was discussed in the chapter on children's reaction to crisis, children may have the most difficulty. Children's reality is often formed by fantasy, partial truths, and an immature ability to discern what is happening around them. They need their own reliable source to listen and to respond effectively to their feelings and concerns.

The group of significant others has been broadened increasingly to include co-workers, schoolmates, teammates, and many others who collectively or individually are impacted by a crisis situation in their setting. When bad things such as shootings, hostage situations, suicides, injuries, deaths, accidents, and disasters of other types happen in a workplace, a school, a hospital, or a courthouse, the emotional fall out spreads beyond that of the primary victim's family. Suddenly and unexpectedly, co-workers and fellow students who survive must face their own vulnerability and their personal concerns that the tragedy has triggered. In a matter of minutes their environment has undergone a change. They could have been the primary victim of the shooter, or the hostage taker. Their life could have ended in the mine shaft accident. The situation becomes personal. Increasingly, crisis response teams are brought into these situations to provide emotional first aid as needed.

Thirty Steps for Handling Family Crises

1. Pull together as a family by establishing a sense of purpose.
2. Allow your feelings to be whatever they are; avoid berating yourself for discounting your feelings or those of your children.
3. Let your children talk with you about their fears, concerns, confusion, anger, sadness, and problems.
4. Talk in words your children can understand. Avoid euphemisms.
5. Allow your children to see your grief, and be honest with them about your feelings. Avoid as much gore as possible in your expressions.
6. Don't expect your children to resolve your grief.
7. Reassure your children that they are safe and will be taken care of.
8. Don't be afraid to say that you do not know the answers to your children's questions. Your honesty may make it easier for them to tolerate the ambiguity in their own minds.
9. If a death occurs, share with your children in terms that they can understand.

10. Remember that children often take their lead for their own behavior from their parents. Children will watch and learn how you handle crises.

11. Children will look to you for structure, guidance, limits, and support. Give these things to them.

12. Ask your children what they need from you. Maybe they need a hug, time to talk, play time with you, or straight talk. Children of different ages will need different things at different times. Adapt your actions to your children's ages and levels of maturity.

13. Identify areas of concern in your life over which you have control, and exercise that control.

14. Have realistic expectations of yourself and your children to minimize stress.

15. Be realistic about each child's role in the family.

16. Continue projects that you have begun.

17. Create a routine for yourself, and stick to it.

18. Maintain your personal health and hygiene.

19. Plan outings and activities with friends. This mutual support can be helpful.

20. Set boundaries with your children. Hear their feelings, and understand the behavior that might result from these feelings. Establish limits to provide stability, structure, and continuity. Don't overdo it by being too strict or too lenient.

21. Observe changes in your children's behavior, attitudes, and expressions. Pay attention to both verbal and non verbal behavior. Be prepared to respond as appropriate.

22. Use support groups as necessary for your children and for yourself. Participate separately or together with your children, as appropriate.

23. Obtain professional help for yourself and your children as needed. Sometimes counseling in conjunction with support groups offers maximum benefit.

24. Find something to laugh about each day. Use laughter to assist in managing stress.

25. Walk or exercise regularly, and include sufficient rest and relaxation in your schedule.

26. Both for yourself and for your children, maintain the continuity of the familiar. This includes schedules, school attendance, friendships, TV programs, and regular activities.

27. Listen.

28. Hear.
29. Respond.
30. Model.
31. Don't lecture.

How Parents Can Help Their Children Cope with Crisis-Related Feelings

1. Talk with your child; provide simple, accurate answers to questions.
2. Talk with your child about your own feelings.
3. Listen to what your child says and how he/she says it. Does the child display fear, anxiety, or insecurity? Repeating your child's words can be very helpful. Use phrases such as "You are afraid that . . . " or "You wonder if . . . " This helps both you and your child clarify feelings.
4. Reassure your child. For example, tell him/her, "We are together. I love you and I will take care of you."
5. You may need to repeat information and reassurances to your child many times. Do not stop responding just because you told your child something once.
6. Hold your child. Provide comfort. Touching is important for children during crises.
7. Spend extra time putting your child to bed; talk and offer reassurance. Leave a night-light on if necessary.
8. Observe your child at play. Listen to what your child says, and watch how he/she plays. Frequently children express feelings of fear or anger while playing with dolls, toy trucks, or friends.
9. Provide play experiences to relieve tension. Work with Play-Doh, paint pictures, play in water, or some favorite activity. If children show a need to hit or kick, give them something safe such as a pillow or a ball.
10. If your child has an especially meaningful toy or blanket, allow him/her to rely on it somewhat more than usual.
11. If you need professional assistance, seek it early to maximize the benefits.

Crisis, Stress, and Holiday Celebrations

Holidays, birthdays, and anniversaries all come sooner than we expect. For many people, the prospect of the holidays and of family celebrations is filled with anguish and anxiety. And when these holidays and celebrations take place without that special loved one, they are much harder to get through. Holidays can be accompanied by the emotional battering of anticipatory stress followed by post holiday blues. It can take weeks to recover from the agony of unfilled expectations, the debt resulting from overspending to create the "perfect holiday," and the disappointment of rediscovering that family conflicts and losses remain unresolved despite the promises of holiday music and commercial messages.

Therapists know that holidays are times when patients and clients often turn away from the hard work they have been doing with their counselors and rely on the season, the holiday, or the celebration to do it for them. Loan officers know they will be deluged with requests from people who will "buy now and worry later."

During holiday seasons, loneliness, depression, alienation, stress, exacerbated personal problems and situations, financial problems, disappointment, dissatisfaction, lack of fulfillment, unrealized hopes, aging, loss, fear, gain, anxiety, terror, guilt, and unresolved worry plague many of us. Present perhaps all year long, tensions increase with the expectation that somehow, in some way, the holiday will make it "all better." The season itself does little or nothing to solve the problems in our lives. Yet many of us annually perpetuate the fantasy that this year it will be different. The responsibility for creating emotional comfort rests with the individual, not the season. Changing our belief from "the holiday will make it better" to "I will make it better" is the first major step in managing holiday stress and preventing post holiday let down.

Teachable Moment

The responsibility for creating emotional comfort rests with the individual, not the season or the holiday.

Twenty Steps for Avoiding Holiday Crisis

1. Be realistic in your expectations about holidays and celebrations. Keep the euphemisms about the holiday in balance, and accept things as they are at the moment. Remember that acceptance does not necessarily mean agreement.
2. Remember, it is not what the holiday does for us, but what we do with the holiday that makes the difference. Use these events to build family unity, strengthen the bonds between family members, and remember loved ones who are far away.
3. Recognize that you are responsible for your life and that nothing and no one can be responsible for you. Saying to yourself, "If only Bob were here everything would be OK," merely sidesteps your getting on with your life as necessary.
4. Live year-round, and especially at this season, by the present realities, not by your fantasy of how you want things to be.
5. Look to yourself as the source of your well-being and happiness.
6. Spend realistically. Give realistically. Going into debt will not create a "perfect" holiday or celebration.
7. Put gift giving and tasks in perspective.
8. Recognize your grown children as adults.
9. If necessary, remind you parents that you are an adult.
10. Clarify family expectations long before the holiday season or celebration. Communicate feelings, exchange ideas, discuss arrangements, and check schedules; include all family members as appropriate. Avoid assumptions.
11. If you are planning a visit with your parents, make your expectations clear. Alert your parents about arrangements you might be considering. Avoid assumptions about babysitting, sleeping arrangements, transportation, and so on. "Home for the holidays" can be either a nightmare or a lovely experience. Consideration, fairness, clarity, careful planning, and shared feelings help determine a visit's success.
12. Invite your parents to your home for the holiday.
13. Acknowledge and allow for the feelings you experience. What you feel is very real. Allow yourself to miss loved ones who are away, and allow your children to express their feelings.

14. Remember it is all right to let your children see your feelings; it may help them learn more about handling theirs.
15. Share the work of holiday events. Assuming all the responsibility often results in victimhood.
16. Stick to regular diet and sleep routines as much as possible.
17. Manage your time. Learn to say no when saying yes would be unrealistic.
18. To avoid letdown, plan some interesting activities for after the holidays.
19. If you are in counseling, stay in counseling during the holiday season.
20. Learn to appreciate who and what you have rather than wishing you had someone or something else.
21. Enjoy this particular time of the year, and this particular time of your life. It will never happen again.

Grief, Loss, and Change

The Grief Factor in Crisis Situations

Every crisis situation involves an element of grief. Crisis involves loss, and loss often results in grief. A person grieves over the loss of anything felt to be important in his or her life. If the loss is so great that it totally tears apart the sufferer's sense of well-being, the person will experience crisis. If the loss is felt to be minor, the grieving process might be completed quickly with the person using his or her usual coping mechanisms.

It is important for the intervener to understand that four elements determine the effect of grief on an individual. These are the intensity of the emotions experienced as a result of the loss, the personal value attached to the loss, the perceived long-term effects the loss will have on the person's life, and the person's resiliency to adapt to change.

As in every crisis situation, the significance of the loss is determined by the sufferer. Crisis is always in the eyes of the beholder. The way the victim currently perceives the world is the victim's reality. The intervener must recognize this principle in order to be effective and, thus, helpful to the sufferer.

Consider the following statements made by crisis victims to the intervener:

- "We moved into a brand-new beautiful home last month."
- "My daughter got married last week to a fine young man."
- "Well, I finally retired last week."
- "My company was downsized. I lost my job."
- "My wallet was stolen."
- "My husband was granted sole custody of our kids."
- "My wife died recently."

- "My house was broken into yesterday."
- "I can't find the paper napkin." The victim is 4 years old.
- "I found out yesterday that I have breast cancer."
- "My bird died this morning."
- "My husband's military unit is probably going to deploy soon."
- "I used to love my husband."

The first three situations might seem to evoke positive reactions. The final ten situations might seem to evoke sad reactions. All the statements are repeated below. This time, under each individual statement is an additional statement that identifies the crisis. This information was provided during the assessment phase of the intervention.

- "We moved into a brand new beautiful home last month."
  Crisis: I did not want to change my life. I did not want to leave my friends, my neighbors, my garden that I spent eight years developing. I feel like a trapped stranger and I want to go back to my real home. Now! I have never felt like this. My husband and daughter are upset with my attitude.
- "My daughter got married last week to a fine young man."
  Crisis: I dreaded this day since the engagement was announced. Now the day has come. My little girl has left the nest. The family unit is disrupted and I can't stand it.
- "Well, I finally retired last week."
  Crisis: I worked at that company for 40 years. I was top dog there. Now I'm just another nobody.
- "My company downsized. I lost my job."
  Crisis: What am I going to do? Maybe my wife could go to work. In my culture, it is not accepted for the woman to work and certainly not to earn more than the man. I will lose respect. I am so torn up.
- "My wallet was stolen."
  Crisis: No. I wasn't physically harmed. What I cherished most was taken from me. I can't replace some special family pictures that I always keep with me.
- "My husband was granted sole custody of our kids."
  Crisis: My kids are going to think I did not fight hard enough to keep them. They are going to think I don't love them. That kills me. I won't get over that loss.
- "My wife died recently."
  Crisis: I am so lonely. I'm so lost. Nothing helps.

- "My house was broken into yesterday."
  Crisis: I feel violated and very vulnerable.
- "I can't find the paper napkin."
  Crisis: My daddy drew my picture on it before the car killed him.
- "I found out that I have breast cancer."
  Crisis: They are going to operate. I'm losing part of my body. I'm in shock.
- "My bird died this morning."
  Crisis: It's not really the bird. He was kind of a nuisance. It's that I cannot handle another death, another loss, another change.
- "My husband's military unit is probably going to deploy to Iraq soon."
  Crisis: I already have all these terrible fears about what is going to happen to him and to us. I have nightmares.
- "I used to love my husband."
  Crisis: My husband refuses to discuss his physical condition with me. The condition was diagnosed two years ago. He's in and out of the hospital. He's totally self-absorbed and gets angry when I try to talk to him or help him. I feel like Alice in Wonderland. Everything is off balance.

The above 13 situations vary in facts, but the responses of the sufferers reflect similar feelings of sadness/fear/anxiety/disbelief/helplessness/guilt/longing/disruption/loneliness/isolation that often accompanies loss and/or change. The grief is experienced at a personal level.

The link between a sufferer's grief and an incident such as a death, dying, illness, accidents, or disasters presents few difficulties for the intervener. As a society, we understand these situations and we grieve when these events occur. Difficult to deal with is the weight that society places on marriage, a pregnancy, moving into a new home, a promotion, and retirement. The universal expectation is that these events will be the highlights of one's life. Often well-meaning friends, relatives, and associates add to the unrealistic hype. Interveners must avoid this trap. They must be observant, they must listen, they must not assume anything, and they must separate their own needs, beliefs, and feelings from those of the victim when they attempt to mitigate the crisis.

This is an excellent opportunity to underscore what was stated in Chapter 3 regarding communications. All communications contain three messages: a content message, a feeling message, and a meaning message. Had the intervener in the first three crisis situations not been alert, he or she might have heard the content message and assumed this was not a crisis situation. He might have congratulated the first woman on her brand-new beautiful home, wished the second woman well on her daughter's marriage to a fine man, and congratulated the gentleman on his recent retirement. The intervener would have failed to hear the feelings and concerns that were simmering below the surface. The result: this would have closed down the communications and exacerbated the crisis.

1. Encourage and allow sufferers to express emotions, without judging them.

MR. JONES: *I retired a month ago after 35 years at the same company.*
INTERVENER: *I see such sadness in your eyes.*
MR. JONES: *I can't stop crying. It's like my whole world just stopped. . . . I feel so ashamed because everyone keeps telling me how lucky I am now that I can do anything that I want. I want to go back to being somebody. I want to feel important and alive! I'm just waiting to die.*

2. Let sufferers take the time necessary to express feelings before addressing options.

INTERVENER: *Mr. Smith, you said that no one understands what you are going through.*
MR. SMITH: *I've been offered a partnership within an aggressive, well-established firm.*
INTERVENER: *What does that offer mean to you?*
MR. SMITH: *A lot more pain. You see, I'll have to move to the West Coast.*
INTERVENER: *And what does that mean?*
MR. SMITH: *I just went through a bad divorce. . . . I lost my wife, the house, a lot of things important to me. My parents live here now. This move means giving up more things and more people. . . . Financially I can't afford not to go . . . but I can't give up anything more . . .*

INTERVENER: *I hear how hard this decision is for you. There are lots of feelings about moving and giving things up that are important to you.*

3. Assure sufferers that their emotions are normal and acceptable.

MRS. BROWN: *My husband died six weeks ago. I don't think I want to go on any more either.*

INTERVENER: *I'm sorry for your pain, Mrs. Brown. What do you need right now?*

MRS. BROWN: *You're the only one who has asked me that. Everyone else is so busy telling me what I should do and what I should feel. I have had to be brave so I wouldn't hurt anyone's feelings or worry my children. I'm about to crack up!*

INTERVENER: *It's hard to keep up appearances.*

MRS. BROWN: *Please, just let me be me for a little while. Just let me be me.*

INTERVENER: *Take your time. I'm here.*

4. Assure sufferers that they can live through a lonely, painful experience.

INTERVENER: *I hear the pain. I don't know exactly what you are experiencing, but I know you are hurting a great deal. I know you can get through this. It is OK to take baby steps.*

5. Let sufferers talk about feelings of guilt that might be associated with the crisis. Accept the validity of the guilt feelings just as you do the validity of other feelings expressed.

INTERVENER: *Is there another piece that I am missing?*

JACK: *Well. This is hard. I've known about the lump for a few months. I didn't say anything to my mom because I was scared.*

INTERVENER: *Tell me what you planned to do.*

JACK: *Well. I pretended it would just go away. I hid the letter that came from the doctor. I just denied it was a problem. I guess I'm lucky that my mom finally found out.*

6. Allow sufferers to express anger and resentment about the loss. Assure them that these feelings are normal.

7. Remain caring, interested, and nonjudgmental.

8. Reach out to sufferers in appropriate ways.

9. Reach out physically only with permission.

What Sufferers Might Experience During the Grief Process

Feeling off balance
Dizziness
Feeling uncoordinated
Erratic appetite
Disturbed sleep patterns
Feeling drugged without having taken drugs or medication
Feeling "out of sync" with one's own body
Irritability
Anger
Feeling disconnected from family, friends, and associates
Feeling disoriented
Rage from deep within one's own body
Feeling as if one is "falling apart" physically and emotionally
Feeling out of control
Deep sadness
Hopelessness
Feeling unwilling and/or incapable of making decisions
Feeling that nothing has meaning and nothing matters
Feeling frozen in time and space
Feeling that all activity, no matter how limited is too much effort
Confusion
Embarrassment about feelings
Guilt
An overwhelming sense of panic that nothing will ever feel right
   again
Feeling of spinning around but getting nowhere
Resentment that the loss has occurred
Relief that the ordeal leading to the final loss is over, and then guilt
   at feeling relieved

Feeling empty
Feeling numb
Feeling pushed down, buried, and very small
Turmoil associated with new or competing emotions
Ambivalence
Euphoria one moment and depression the next

Self-Intervention for Sufferers

Interveners should help the sufferers do the following:

1. Avoid major changes that will require being uprooted physically or emotionally from loved ones, support systems, and that which is familiar and safe.
2. Put major decisions on hold.
3. Rely on the security of the familiar.
4. Set realistic expectations concerning work, home, chores, family obligations, and all other areas of life.
5. Seek out those people who are helpful and comforting and avoid, where possible, those who exacerbate the sufferer's discomfort. Being well-intentioned does not necessarily translate into helpful behavior.
6. Recognize that the death of a significant other creates a sense of helplessness in survivors. Sufferers should identify those areas of life over which they have control and exercise that control immediately.
7. Maintain a daily routine. Persons suffering from grief should get up, get dressed, get out, and get moving every morning. This helps give the sufferer a sense of purpose and direction.
8. Care for themselves as follows:
   a. If work schedules do not permit rest during the day, arrange a routine after or before work to allow for extra rest as needed.
   b. Take appropriate vitamins to supplement the diet and minimize stress.
   c. Exercise daily to relieve tension.
   d. Walk daily and allow the senses of touch, smell, feeling, hearing, and sight to be energizers.
9. Let the process of recovery take as long as it takes.
10. Discover and use personal strengths.

Coping with Separation and the Unknown

Interveners should help sufferers do the following:

1. Concentrate on the present.
2. Avoid trying to focus on the distant future.
3. Live for today.
4. Enjoy family and social relationships, and allow talk about thoughts and feelings as needed.
5. Finish projects previously started. If none are in progress, start a project and find enjoyment in it. Build for success by setting a reasonable, doable pace.
6. View each day as a victory.
7. Remember that each of us copes in different ways. People should find the best way by listening to their needs.
8. Accept personal responsibility for life as a way of helping oneself.
9. Participate actively in daily routines. Routines help return a sense of structure and purpose.
10. Set realistic goals.
11. Reach out to others and let them know the sufferer's wants.
12. Accept responsibility for their own attitudes, approaches, and frames of reference.
13. Set the tone for others with whom they associate.
14. Work with family, friends, and co-workers to help build and maintain a sense of control, purpose, and hope.
15. Encourage honest, open communications.

A Teachable Moment

The authors have inserted alerts within several chapters of this book. These are labeled as "a mistaken assumption" or "a teachable moment." The authors' purpose is to hone in on issues that are routinely missed. The following should be read and remembered.

There is no shortcut in the grieving process. The sufferer grieves on his or her own internal schedule. There is no such thing as "getting over this pain," a phrase commonly used in an attempt to encourage the sufferer. A more realistic goal is to get through it. Managing to get through the pain usually happens as a result of one's taking baby steps during the early grieving process. It helps to recognize that the process does not follow a smooth path. A person may be moving forward and suddenly reverse course when certain memories or feelings intrude. These interruptions may be uncomfortable but they are normal and will likely happen again. The victim begins to recognize the pitfalls, learns to manage the discomfort, allows for his or her feelings to be whatever they are, takes care of him- or herself, and recovers at his or her own pace. Slowly, slowly one heals. Often the reminder to take baby steps is the most important message that the victim remembers.

Feelings Associated with Dying

The discussion in this chapter has been about grief, loss, and change in numerous situations. The focus will now center on several aspects of death and dying. The following are some of the feelings associated with dying:

1. Anxiety
2. Apathy
3. Paralyzing uncertainty
4. Deep sadness
5. Nameless feelings only as free-floating anxiety
6. Fear of not fulfilling the expectations of those providing care to him or her
7. Helplessness
8. Fear of failure
9. Guilt
10. Grief
11. Depression
12. A feeling of urgency to experience a sense of closure
13. A sense of separation and disintegration
14. Loss of control over body and environment
15. Increasing dependency
16. Threat of abandonment, isolation, and desertion
17. Concern that the expression of emotion will result in abandonment by family and medical attendants
18. Fear that expression of tenderness, love, and intimacy may cause significant others additional grief and anguish

19. Elation about transition to a "better place" or "going to heaven to be with God or other family members"
20. Relief that suffering will soon end
21. Despair in response to losses resulting from the illness—loss of vocation, loss of the ability to participate in usual activities, losses sustained through the process of physical deterioration, sense of interpersonal loss, and the loss of body parts or changes in body image related to the illness
22. Urgency to resolve unfinished business
23. Frustration that reduced level of physical and emotional energy will not allow resolution of unfinished business
34. Concern about talking with the doctor about issues connected with dying. The feelings might be shared more easily with a nurse, a clergyman, or another intervener
35. Hostility toward family and medical staff
36. Envy and jealousy of healthy peers
37. Rage
38. Resentment over not being part of the decision procession
39. Frustration with those who will not give him or her permission to die

Intervention Procedure

The following are guidelines for intervening with a dying person who is in crisis:

Establish rapport with the dying person. The intervener must convey an attitude of understanding and acceptance of the victim.

Listen to what the victim is saying. Encourage him or her to state the problem as he or she perceives it.

Find out what the victim is doing to manage the crisis.

Provide the victim with accurate and complete information concerning his or her condition.

1. Hiding information, giving only partial information, and being unwilling to acknowledge the patient's need to know will often increase the tensions and stresses and potentiate crisis. What may appear to be thoughtful protection of the victim is in fact counterproductive to the intervention process.

2. Include the dying person in the decision-making process to the extent that he or she is willing and able to be included. Often the crisis is the result of the dying person's feelings of impotence, loss of control, and loss of autonomy. Suddenly everyone is arranging his or her life—the family, the doctors and other medical staff, and strangers. The person's feelings of rage, helplessness, and mortality may heighten to crisis proportion.

3. The intervener must deal with the victim's need for involvement in decision making about his or her medical treatment, personal affairs, housing arrangements (private home or institutional setting), and other matters that require arrangements. The intervener may find it necessary to work with the family in helping them understand the importance of the victim's participation in confronting these issues. The intervener should encourage the family to deal with their own feelings in relation to the dying process. The intervener should be prepared to intervene with the family and significant others as needed.

4. Recognize the dying person's need to be alone or his or her need for the physical presence of an intervener only.

5. Be sensitive to both the verbal and the nonverbal messages given by the victim.

6. Be alert for signs of serious depression such as loss of appetite, severe problems of sleep, marked withdrawal from any pleasurable activity, loss of all sexual interests, extreme agitation, and suicidal ideation. The degree of depression is likely to vary considerably over the course of the illness and is related to the degree of loss perceived at the moment. It is important that the intervener be aware that there are times in the dying process when the person does withdraw into himself or herself to quietly work through the intense feelings related to the loss. At other times a withdrawal is the result of a lack of energy to engage in a relationship.

7. Constantly evaluate and re-evaluate the physical and emotional elements of the victim's adaptation to dying.

8. Assist the victim to use his or her remaining resources to maintain meaning in his or her attempt to cope with dying.

9. Continue to show respect for the dying person and take seriously his or her needs and concerns. Allow the person to make a transition from life to death with dignity.

Before attempting to manage the sufferer's grief, the intervener must have acknowledged his or her own feelings concerning dying and death. The fine line between adaptation to the grief process and maladaptive behavior seems to result in the failure to work through the grief process. Denial of feelings, inability to verbalize concerns, lack of clarity in formulating plans, and unexpressed fears of isolation contribute to the state of crisis. During the course of working with the dying patient, the intervener experiences similar feelings of mortality and grief. Unless interveners can feel comfortable with their own feelings about death or at least feel comfortable feeling uncomfortable, they cannot create a setting conducive to allow the victim to begin the grief work.

The Crisis Revisited: Coping with the Aftermath

For many, a crisis can stir painful memories of previous crises. The crisis victims are required to deal with feelings that either were never resolved or were thought to have been resolved. The emotional wounds seem fresh. The anniversary date of a crisis can be difficult for some. People often begin to feel a sense of free-floating anxiety several days before the anniversary date. Acknowledge the feelings; talk about your feelings with a trusted significant other; utilize the coping skills acquired from the previous crisis situation. If that is not effective, seek help from a professional.

Legal Implications of Crisis Intervention[1]

Although Crisis Intervention and the intervener's function is not about the legalities involved, one should at least consider how these legalities relate to intervention. We live in a litigious society, where self-responsibility is often lacking and lawsuits are often the remedy. Lawsuits can be filed against anyone, at almost any time and for almost any reason if a plaintiff feels that a personal wrong or injury has been caused. Generally such claims are brought under civil or tort law rather than under criminal law. That is, civil offenses or torts have been committed against individuals rather than against the state.

Nothing said here can completely prevent such action or insulate the intervener from all exposure. However, some guidelines, procedures, and areas of awareness can ease the potential legal burden of the intervener and allow everyone to get on with the real job—effective assistance to those in crisis.

Not all areas of concern to interveners will be dealt with extensively in this chapter. All interveners, however, should be familiar with the following issues and how the laws regarding these issues apply to them.

Interveners may need to do individual research to ascertain the information they need. For that purpose, legal references are provided at the end of this chapter. The following are some issues that may apply to interveners:

Negligence
Informed consent
Confidentiality

[1]Nothing stated in this chapter should be construed in any way to be legally definitive or to replace your own research into the laws of your state and city. Nor should you take this information as legal advice or as negation of the importance of seeking competent counsel from a licensed attorney.

Exceptions to confidentiality
Duty to warn
Record keeping
Right to privacy
Right to refuse intervention
Good Samaritan laws
Standards of care
Abandonment
Consent to intervention
Actual consent
Implied consent

To work effectively in the Crisis Intervention field, interveners must recognize that they are bound by the laws of society and that, even under extreme circumstances, such proscriptions cannot be ignored without consequence. Good Samaritan laws generally protect those whose intent is to assist others in times of crisis. Such assistance must always be reasonable and prudent and must be based on the level and kind of training the intervener has received and now applies. To such standards of care we must adhere.

For example, the Good Samaritan Law of the State of Texas (Chapter 74 of the Civil Practice and Remedies Code, 2000) states that

(a) A person who in good faith administers emergency care, including using an automated external defibrillator at the scene of an emergency but not in a hospital or other health care facility or means of medical support is not liable in civil damages for an act performed during the emergency unless the act is willfully or wantonly negligent.

(b) This section does not apply to care administered:
   (1) for or in expectation of remuneration; or
   (2) by a person who was at the scene of the emergency because he or a person he represents as an agent was soliciting business or seeking to perform a service for remuneration.

Similar Good Samaritan laws exist in many other states. Interveners should be familiar with the content of the law that applies to them.

Unless an intervener has a preexisting duty to intervene in another person's crisis, the law does not require that anyone intervene in the crisis of anyone else. Police, firefighters, and emergency service personnel usually have a preexisting duty because they are hired to perform such tasks. Further, once an intervener has begun an intervention with another person, the intervention must continue unless the intervener is relieved by someone with greater competency. Not to do so could be construed as abandonment and could expose the intervener to legal consequences.

The courts generally determine liability, so all interveners should understand the concepts of negligence, or malpractice, for which the courts might hold interveners liable. In Crisis Intervention, good intentions are often not enough to avoid legal problems.

Negligence could result when an intervener assumes a duty of reasonable care for a victim and then breaches that duty, thereby causing damage or further injury to the victim. Generally, except when interveners have a preexisting duty, they are not required to intervene with a victim. Their moral or ethical values may dictate otherwise, however.

If an intervener, with or without a preexisting duty, decides to intervene with a sufferer, the intervener may assume a duty of reasonable care for that sufferer. Further, such a duty may be seen as assumed if the intervener acts in a way that creates a foreseeable risk to the victim.

For example, an intervener decides to take action to assist a sufferer. The action resulting from that decision creates a foreseeable risk to the victim; that is, the intervener's action could adversely affect the victim. In this case, the intervener has assumed a duty of reasonable care. If the usual procedure in this particular intervention is to remove the victim from the crisis situation, and the intervener decides against such movement, such a decision might cause additional injury to the victim.

If, as a result of such action, the victim is injured further or is damaged in other ways, the intervener may be said to have breached the duty of reasonable care and to have acted negligently. In such a case, a court might be asked to decide the intervener's liability based on the damages caused. Generally, the measure of negligence the court applies will be the standard of care given by the intervener. It must also be shown that the intervener's actions are the proximate or direct cause of the injury that the sufferer sustains.

Conversely, should the intervener decide not to intervene, lack of action would not create a duty of reasonable care because the intervener's actions—or inaction—would not have created risk to the victim other than that already experienced by the victim at that time. Even though inaction might allow the victim's suffering to continue, no duty of reasonable care has been created because in this case there is no duty to rescue. For police, firefighters, and emergency medical service personnel, however, the opposite may be true because of their preexisting duty to act in such cases.

Legal Guidelines in Crisis Intervention

The following guidelines are intended to help interveners avoid the difficulties of legal confrontations and to keep interveners where they belong, doing what they are best trained to do—serving in the field, helping victims manage the crises in their lives.

1. Always treat people as human beings, not just as cases.
2. Show respect to all with whom you are involved.
3. Intervene within the limits of your background and training. Do not exceed those limits, thereby committing the illegal practice of medicine, law, or psychology.
4. Unless you have a preexisting duty to intervene, consider carefully whether you want to perform an intervention.
5. Once you have begun to intervene, don't stop.
6. Discontinue your intervention only if you are relieved by someone with greater skill than your own.
7. Determine how the Good Samaritan laws relate to the types of intervention in which you may be involved.
8. If in doubt about your legal standing, contact a competent attorney and discuss your concerns.
9. Maintain confidentiality of all information you obtain about a crisis victim. Understand under what special circumstances you may have a duty to warn another person or to otherwise breach intervener–victim confidentiality.
10. Document everything you say and do with a victim. This may assist you later if you or your procedures are challenged.
11. Maintain your competency. Update your training and credentials as required.
12. Whenever possible, obtain the victim's consent before you assist with the crisis. If in doubt, ask!
13. If emergency circumstances do not allow for actual consent by the victim, you may be able to proceed under the concept of implied consent. In such circumstances, however, do only what is absolutely necessary to effectively intervene or rescue.

14. Do not disturb a crime scene. If you cannot avoid doing so, note exact locations of whatever is moved so that later you can give such information to proper authorities.
15. If you must search a victim's personal effects, try to have one or two witnesses present to observe your actions.
16. Know what you are required to report to the authorities. Requirements vary from state to state. (For example, child abuse must be reported in most states.)
17. Know the legal procedures in your jurisdiction for admissions for psychiatric care. Usually admissions are categorized as either voluntary or involuntary.
18. Remember that crisis interveners are not usually immune from observation of motor vehicle laws or from legal responsibility for vehicular accidents or property damage.
19. Respect the victim's right to privacy.
20. If the victim is a minor, obtain the permission of one of the parents before intervening. If this is not possible, you may be able to proceed under the doctrine of implied consent, as you would with an adult.
21. Be honest and open with victims.
22. Always think through what you will do, toward what end you will be doing it, what risks are present, and what safeguards you will apply.
23. Prepare yourself with knowledge of the law as well as of Crisis Intervention skills.
24. Remember that both acts of commission and acts of omission can affect liability.
25. Respect a sufferer's right to refuse your intervention.
26. Before entering a crisis victim's domain, dwelling, or office, request that person's permission. Know when the laws of your locality permit you to enter without permission.
27. If you are the director or supervisor of a Crisis Intervention agency, be sure all interveners and hot-line workers understand and can apply agency policies and procedures.
28. Within Crisis Intervention agencies, develop specific, understandable policies and procedures that clearly regulate and illustrate how intervention is to be performed.
29. As an agency director or supervisor, adhere to agency policy and insist that interveners do likewise.

30. Incorporate agency policies and legal issues into the training of crisis interveners.

Legal References

The reader will find these references beneficial:

Arizona Revised Statute for Privileged Communications, § 32-2085 (1965). (Privileged Communications)

Buwa v. Smith, 84-1905 NMB (1986). (Duty to Warn)

Canterbury v. Spense, 464 F. 2d. 772 (D.C. Cir. 1972), cert. den. 93 S.Ct. 560 (1972). (Informed Consent)

Cutter v. Brownbridge, Cal. Ct. App., 1st Dist. 330 (1986). (Privileged Communications)

Hales v. Pittman, 118 Ariz. 305, 576 P. 2d. 493 (1978). (Informed Consent)

McDonald v. Clinger, 446 N.Y.S. 2d. 801 (1982). (Confidentiality)

McIntosh v. Milano, 403 A. 2d. 500 (N.J.S.Ct. 1979). (Duty to Warn)

New Jersey Revised Statutes, New Jersey Marriage Counseling Act, Annotated § 45: 8B-29 (1969). (Exceptions to Confidentiality)

People v. District Court, City and County of Denver, 719 P. 2d. 722 (Colo. 1986). (Privileged Communications)

Rodriguez v. Jackson, 118 Ariz. 13, 574 P. 2d. 481 (App. 1978). (Informed Consent)

Sard v. Hardy, 291 Md. 432, 379 A. 2d. 1014 (1977). (Informed Consent)

Tarasoff v. Regents of California, 131 Cal. Rptr. 14, 551 P. 2d. 334 (1976). (Duty to Warn)

Whitree v. State of New York, 56 Misc. 2d. 693, 290 N.Y.S. 2s. 486 (1968). (Record Keeping)

Disasters

These are voices of men, women, and children after surviving tsunamis/earthquakes/hurricanes/tornados/forest fires/floods/industrial accidents/derailments/terrorist attacks/suicides/homicide/war. The sites of the disaster events are global. The psychological fallout is also global.

MAN: *Now I have no family. Now I have no neighbors. I have no home. I have no work. I have nothing. . . . Why should I go on? Why bother? Why? . . . Give me a reason why . . .*

WOMAN: *I am waiting for my children to come back to me from the water . . .*

WOMAN: *I must have my husband's body to bury . . . even just an arm . . . some part of him that I can bury and say a prayer over . . . and I can know where he rests.*

CHILD: *Why won't Mommy answer me? Is she angry at me?*

MAN: *How can I reach some government official? I am a tourist. My passport, wallet, and tickets were destroyed. I need information. I need help immediately. Please help.*

MAN: *I was holding my little baby. He was blown out of my arms by the strong winds. He is gone. . . . I'm alive and he is gone! I can never be forgiven for this. . . . I am going crazy!*

WOMAN: *Out of nowhere came a plane. It was a normal day. Sunny, quiet, uneventful. I was at work. I went outside for a break. All of a sudden a plane was heading directly toward my building. It was so sudden and so unexpected. I can't get it out of my head.*

These are scenes from the disasters:

Children whose eyes are devoid of expression.

Survivors wandering like zombies through the rubble and the devastation.

Women huddled together trying to console one another.

Some people crying, some rocking back and forth shaking their heads, some trying to restore order within the chaos.

Medics tending to crying children.

People staring out at the water as if trying to will back their lives and their loved ones.

Devastation, rubble, debris, some intact structures, fallen trees, damaged vehicles, charred remains, flooded streets and homes, bodies in various states of repose, looting.

Children playing sports with whatever equipment they can find; lost young children latching on to the skirts of a kind stranger.

Emergency Response Teams Doing Their Best in Unfamiliar, Chaotic Circumstances.

What has been the public's reaction as we have watched disaster scenes and listened to the many voices during media reports? How have our colleagues and our associates been affected? Have we vicariously become victims of the numerous disasters? Examples of the comments the authors hear:

Events are piling on . . . suicide bombings, hurricanes, earthquakes, shootings, terrorists. I feel so sad and tired all the time

Those children in Indonesia and Haiti—I can't sleep. I can't concentrate. I'm afraid to let my children go anywhere by themselves. I have never felt this way before.

I feel so helpless lately. It's like I don't really have control. Everything around us feels scary and I can't protect my family from it.

My dad used to talk about a pervasive feeling of malaise—when you are not sick, but you are not well either. That describes me.

I am waiting for the other shoe to drop.

A continuum of natural and man-made disasters seem to define the "new normal."

Prepare to Respond to a Disaster

Crisis intervention during man-made or natural disasters is similar to crisis intervention done in other venues. It differs mainly in that whatever is done must be done for more victims over a longer period of time and usually under extremely difficult circumstances for both the victims and the responders. Terrain, accessibility, weather conditions, reliability of equipment, sufficiency of food and supplies, and communication capabilities are just some of the issues that raise concerns for responders. Those who choose to respond to disasters must possess specific training, resilience, and stamina. Be alert to the following:

1. Prepare. Prepare.
2. Obtain the specific types of training that will allow you to function in your area.
3. Expect to function as part of a team.
4. Know your chain of command.
5. Understand the Incident Command System.
6. Understand and develop triage skills.
7. Know the meaning of triage under disaster conditions and that it may be different than non-disaster conditions.
8. Know physical first aid in addition to emotional first aid.
9. If you are not called to intervene, don't show up unannounced.
10. Work in teams of at least two interveners.
11. Practice. Practice.
12. Maintain your certifications as required.
13. Prepare by learning about the effects of disaster on those experiencing it.
14. Expect disasters to be unpleasant.
15. Remember that there is really no panacea for stress reactions in times of disaster or terror events.
16. Recognize the interplay between distress responses, behavioral changes, and psychiatric stress during a disaster or terror event.
17. Recognize that risk factors will increase psychological problems based on degree of exposure, the level of exhaustion, physical harm that has occurred, and the presence of a preexisting mental disorder.

18. The scene of a disaster may present as a scary and terrifying place to all including crisis interveners. Prepare for this. Most of us do not operate in these conditions on a daily basis. Be ready for that which you really do not expect or that in which you do not want to be.

19. Understand what Weapons of Mass Destruction are.

20. Understand what Weapons of Mass Effect are.

21. Know that CBRNE stands for Chemical release, Biological release, Radiological event, Nuclear detonation, and Explosive devices or incidents. You will hear these terms.

22. The greatest challenges for a civilian caught in a catastrophic situation are often:
    a. No personal protection equipment.
    b. Fear and anxiety.
    c. Cultural issues that may hinder aid.
    d. Keeping families together—don't forget this.

23. Risk perception may be affected by:
    a. The fact that the threat may be invisible.
    b. The fact that the threat may be odorless.
    c. The exposure and uncertainties; long-term effects.
    d. Multiple unexplained symptoms. Headaches, nausea, and fatigue are examples.
    e. Unfamiliarity with disaster situations that depart widely from non disaster scenarios.
    f. Grotesqueness.
    g. Moral outrage.

24. Mass panic is unusual. Historically, it is not a common reaction to a disaster.

25. Panic may be the result of a serious perceived threat combined with limited or no avenues of escape for the victims.

26. Perceived threats do not have to be real to affect the victim. Reality is always in the eye of the beholder. If the victim or the sufferer thinks that it is real, it is real to that person. Never try to talk someone out of their perceptions. It cannot be done and it demonstrates your lack of understanding.

28. Remember when involved in disaster response:
    a. Eat when you can.
    b. Sleep when you can.
    c. Go to the bathroom when you can.

Take Care of Yourself

Many times, disaster personnel experience feelings of guilt if they take time for themselves, if they take time to eat, and if they have food when others do not. If you do not take care of yourself, you will not be able to care for or about someone else. Taking care of one's self including physical care and psychological care is essential in maintaining resilience and stamina. Acute care crisis intervention for victims is the basis of psychological force protection for responders. Take care of yourself. Take care of your co-responders. Take care of the victims.

1. Plan to take care of yourself and to provide for your own needs.
2. Assemble personal gear that will allow you to subsist over extended time periods.
3. Put together a "go bag" with your professional resource information and tools of the trade that you might need to use with victims of a disaster. Hand puppets, Gumby, or a picture book weigh little and can be helpful in responding to kids.
4. Be able to function on your own. Travel light. Consider the terrain.
5. Prepare yourself to detect and to respond to hazards, physical and psychological.
6. Know when you need to take a time out.
7. Keep a watchful eye on your co-workers.
8. Know what to stay away from. This is as important as knowing what to get involved in.
9. Approach all scenes and victims with great care and caution.
10. Use your equipment sparingly. You may need to assist many.
11. Be prepared to ask for assistance if you need it.
12. Know from where your back-up is coming.
13. Wear appropriate personal protective equipment.
14. Learn to trust your equipment.
15. Understand the effects of vicarious trauma and compassion fatigue. All interveners are vulnerable.
16. Learn steps to take to manage your own stress.
17. Know the signs of stress in yourself. Watch for them.
18. Understand the limitations of your own body and mind under disaster conditions.
19. Take care of your own personal hygiene when time allows.

20. Crisis Interveners are not supermen or superwomen. Don't pretend you are.
21. Let your family and loved ones know where you are and that you are okay.
22. Accept that interveners can have the same symptoms of psychological response as others. This includes veteran interveners.
23. Try to always work with a "buddy." Working alone may not be safe or secure.
24. You cannot be all things to all people. Know what you can do and do that. If you give all of yourself to every victim, you will have nothing left to give.
25. Rely on your support systems just as you advise others to rely on theirs.

Apply Crisis Intervention Procedure

What is most often needed in the early stages of a disaster is crisis management. Not crisis treatment or crisis resolution, but crisis management. This involves such things as, but are not limited to, structure, answers, honesty, direction, and guidance. The model may vary according to style and training, but the goal is the same.

1. Understand and respond to the timeliness of a crisis.
2. Remember that crises are self-limiting.
3. Remember that crises are time-limited.
4. Understand that most reactions to a crisis or disaster situation are normal, to be expected, and usual under the circumstances.
5. Know the threats presented by your particular situation.
6. Adjust to the reality that you cannot attend to or preserve every victim.
7. Learn to accept that some victims will die or will be dead when you arrive there.
8. Encourage self-reliance among victims.
9. Follow the model for crisis intervention of Immediacy, Control, Assessment, Disposition, Referral, and Follow-up.
10. Remember that different people may respond differently to the same situation.

11. Accept your duty to normalize.
12. Educate others so that panic will not ensue.
13. Exude confidence even though you might be scared yourself.
14. Although you will be involved with victims, acknowledge problem ownership.
15. Avoid overidentification with victims. They need your help, not your pity.
16. Recognize symptoms of psychological stress such as anger, self-blame, isolation, withdrawal, blaming, fear, feeling stunned, variations in mood, feelings of helplessness, the tendency to deny, memory problems, family discord, sadness, and grief.
17. Recognize the physiological symptoms such as limited or no appetite, chest pains, body aches, headaches, gastrointestinal problems, hyperactivity, drug and/or alcohol abuse or misuse, trouble getting to sleep or staying asleep, troubled dreams and nightmares, and low energy levels and fatigue even after rest or sleep.
18. Provide stress inoculations for interveners. Previous experience in successfully handling stressful situations often acts as an inoculation in that it prepares the intervener when they encounter the next stressful situation.
19. Emphasize the team approach.
20. Force fluids for interveners.
21. Use fluids as indicated for victims.
22. Remember that responses of victims may be mediated by cognitive functioning, physical health, personal relationships, duration and intensity of normal life disruption, personal meaning attached to the disaster or related events, the usual psychological well-being of the victim pre-crisis, and by elapsed time since the disaster occurred.
23. Always perform an immediate assessment of victims or sufferers when encountered.
24. Enlist assistance of those able to be of help.
25. Support those who need support.
26. Listen. Listen.
27. Help victims to reconnect with usual and normal support systems.
28. Expect that victims may need help accessing support systems.

29. Be cautious in offering advice to sufferers.
30. Provide the needed psychological structure for a victim.
31. Provide the needed physical structure for a victim.
32. Be reliable in what you say you will do.
33. Return control of the victim's life to the victim as quickly as they are able to exercise the control.
34. Do not say that you understand exactly how the victim feels.
35. Remember that your credibility as an intervener is continually being evaluated by the victim.
36. Do not tell victims to stop feeling what they feel.
37. Do not tell victims that they should not feel the way that they feel.
38. Do not tell a victim not to cry. Do not challenge perceptions of the victims. Crisis is always in the eye of the beholder.
39. Never say that you don't think that things are really as bad as the victim says they are.
40. Be careful that your responses to victims do not elicit negative responses or reactions to your intervention. Credibility is at issue.
41. Be respectful of a victim and his or her needs.
42. Triage those with abnormal responses separately from those with normal responses.
43. Treat within the scope of your competency and resources.
44. Identify those at high risk for immediate referral and treatment.
45. Normalize responses.
46. Empathize with victims.
47. Reduce psychological arousal.
48. Access support for the most distressed victims.
49. Screen for depression and suicide.
50. Ask if the victim has felt depressed: have they lost interest in things they would normally have interest in; have they had thoughts that their life was not worth living; and have they had recent thoughts about killing themselves.
51. Assess suicidal possibilities by focusing on the lethality of the means and the specificity of the plan.
52. Assess for stress disorders by assessing startle responses, emotional numbing, emotional arousal or emotional avoidance, and the persistence of the symptoms.

53. Assess victims for possibilities of alcohol or substance abuse by asking if they felt that they should cut down; have others annoyed them by telling them to cut down on drinking; have they felt guilty about their own drinking; and do they routinely need a drink to start the day in order to overcome a hangover.
54. Those involved may present with many symptoms.
55. Symptoms presented may not be expected.
56. Watch your sufferers for signs of agents to include nausea, muscle aches, respiratory problems, unusual fatigue, and dizziness.
57. Expect many questions about certainty of exposure or degree of exposure.
58. Try to respond to questions about long-term effects of agents in a realistic manner based on what you actually know rather than on unsubstantiated or rumor information.
59. Expect twice the number of psychological casualties as you have physical casualties.
60. Expect confusion, bewilderment, and the inability to care for self.
61. Expect confusion, anxiety, emotional flailing, and trial-and-error problem-solving behavior.
62. Enlist the aid of victims who want to help. Not everyone will react to the situation in the same way. Some will want and need to do something helpful. Accept their help as appropriate.

"I Need Information"

Often the immediate need victims express is for information. The following is a sampling of the questions often asked:

....When can I go home and check on things?
....When can I get electricity turned on?
....I lost my medication. How can I get a refill?
....How can I get glasses? Mine broke and I can't see much.
....Where is the rest of my family? They left on a different bus.
....Why can't I go home? It's my home.
....Is there a doctor? My kid needs a doctor.
....I don't have any money. What do I do now?

....How can I get word to my family?

....Will my insurance cover this? Is this wind or water damage?

....What is going to happen to us?

....How long will the shelter stay open?

....Where are we going?

....How can I contact my boss?

....Do you have some pills to help me sleep?

....I need my insulin . . . What do I do?

....I want to go stay with my sister in Alabama. Will they help me pay for that?

....Can I sleep in a separate room in the shelter? I'm scattered of strangers.

....Why do I have to evacuate if I don't want to?

....Why is it taking so long?

....Who is in charge?

....Were the schools destroyed?

....Where can I go to the bathroom?

....Are there government offices still open? All my paperwork was destroyed.

....Is anything left? You know, schools, movies, the newspaper, the hospital?

Victims want and need accurate and reliable information. Victims look to the intervener to provide accurate and reliable answers. The intervener's credibility is on the line. Do not make things up. If you don't know the answer, say so. Tell them where, how, or from whom to get the information or, if you can, contact the person yourself to obtain an answer. Some questions will seem silly or irrelevant, but they reflect the concerns of particular victims. Do not patronize or insult victims. They have suffered enough.

A Brief Review of Effective Communication Skills

Disaster situations may bring out old emotional wounds as well as those caused instantly. When this occurs, the following questions can be asked to determine the priority for the intervention:

1. Which of the problems presented is of immediate concern? Which has the highest priority as evaluated by the intervener?

2. Which problem would prove most damaging if not dealt with immediately?
3. Which of the problems presented can be resolved the quickest?
4. Which problem must be dealt with before others can be handled?
5. What resources do I have at hand to handle the problems presented?
6. What are the barriers and obstacles currently present, or likely to be present, that will hinder problem solving?
7. Is there anything that must be done or changed now in order to enhance problem management?

The intervener must be able to acquire the needed information quickly and accurately. While some of the information needed might be provided by external sources, most of it will come directly from the victim. This means that the intervener must listen actively to the victim's total message and give the person full concentration and undivided attention. The intervener must sift through the victim's words to gain information and insight into the person's problems and views of the problems.

Understand the Messages

Every communication from the disaster victim contains three messages:

1. A content message. This message provides information about what the victim believes, thinks, or perceives the situation to be.
2. A feeling message. The feeling message conveys the nature and intensity of the sender's emotion about the current or the related situations.
3. A meaning message. This concerns the behavior or situation that has generated the feeling.
4. Usually, the person who sends the communication implies, rather than explicitly states, the behavior or situation that creates the feelings. The intervener must try to infer what the behavior or situation is.

Understand the Nature of Distortion

Dr. Edward S. Rosenbluh, a pioneer in the field of Crisis Interventions, explained that when another person communicates with you, distortions can occur in three main areas:

1. What the person means to say.
2. What the person actually says.
3. What you, as the disaster responder, believe that you hear.

Be Empathetic

The key to effective listening is accurately hearing the feelings and meaning behind the content of the message of any communication. This is often referred to as empathy. Empathy is the ability to enter the victim's world and to reflect your understanding of this world to the victim. Empathy contains two elements:

1. Passive empathy: This is the ability to hear the facts contained in the words and the feelings contained in the victim's body language—intensity, and tone.
2. Active empathy: Active empathy refers to the ability to reflect this understanding to the other person in a manner that generates warmth and trust. If the responder stays at surface level, the probability exists that the real crisis will not be revealed.

Avoid Making Assumptions

Interveners must not assume that they understand what the victim means. The intervener must know precisely what the victim means. To be certain:

1. Inquire to clarify vague or ambiguous statements.
2. Be sure that the intervener and the victim are talking about the same thing at the same time.

Clarify Statements

1. Repeating key words
   a. Repeat key words or phrases that the victim uses.
   b. Focus on a specific word or phrase that is not clearly understood. This may cause the victim to clarify the meaning.
   c. Encourage the victim to explain in more detail.
   d. Be careful using this technique. Repeating can sound insincere if overly used.
2. Restatement
   a. Rephrase what the victim says as a way of clarifying the meaning.
   b. The additional information gained using this technique will help the intervener to understand what the victim is thinking and feeling.
3. The direct method
   a. Admit that you are confused by the victim's statement.
   b. The victim will know that you are interested in what is being said.
4. Asking questions
   a. Simple way to get a clearer idea of the victim's meaning.
   b. Ask simple questions.
   c. Ask one question at a time.
   d. Ask open-ended questions to gain information.
   e. Ask closed-ended questions to pinpoint specific items. Especially effective when the intervener is fairly sure what additional information is needed.

Know When and How to Ask Questions

1. Pace of questions must be considered so as not to raise the victim's stress level, unless this is desired.
2. Bombarding with questions can confuse and frustrate the victim if not handled well.
3. Allow sufficient time for the victim to answer.
4. Ask in a nonthreatening and nonaccusatory way.

Dealing Effectively with Silence

The intervener will often encounter silence while dealing with crisis disaster victims. Knowing how to handle the silence is very important. For some crisis interveners, silence is deadly. It need not be.

1. Do not assume that silence means that nothing is happening.
2. Learn to be comfortable with your feelings of being uncomfortable.
3. Pay attention to what the victim is "not saying."
4. What significance does this silence have in the overall situation?
5. If the silence persists, you may want to reassure the victim that you are still there and ready to listen if they want to talk.
6. After you reassure the victim, remain quiet.
7. Insert information or empathy into silence only as actually deemed necessary.

Respond to the Victim In an Effective Way

Responding to another person's feelings is a delicate process. In gathering information from victims, interveners must handle feelings with care and concern. If the intervener wants the victim to continue to talk about facts pertinent to the problem, the intervener cannot judge, use logic, or attempt to give advice. The individual's feeling must be legitimized. The goal is to increase communication rather than shut it down.

Use Translators Effectively

The method of using a translator during a disaster or crisis with a non-English–speaking crisis victim is often compromised by lack of proper training for interveners or misunderstandings about effective intervention. Translators serve an important role. Regardless of the language spoken and translated, it must be understood from the outset of the intervention that the crisis intervener must conduct the actual intervention with the victim. This is true even if the translator happens to be a trained intervener.

1. Translators must be chosen carefully prior to an actual incident.
2. Whenever possible, translators should be recruited from reputable agencies that provide such services.
3. In the alternative to an agency, a specific person with the required skills should be sought, evaluated, and trained by the intervention team.
4. The translator acts only as a "word machine" for the crisis intervener.
5. The translator does not conduct the ongoing crisis management with the victim.
6. Translators must be able to say to the sufferer exactly what the intervener says in the same way as the intervener says it.
7. Similarly, he or she must be able to say to the intervener exactly what the victim or sufferer says and in the same way that he or she says it.
8. Translators should not paraphrase what either the victim and intervener says.
9. Information about the victim's tone, inflection, and cultural meanings will be given directly to the intervener if such nuances may not successfully cross cultural borders. The translator should be instructed to do this by the intervener.
10. Translators should not add personal interpretations about what the victim or intervener is saying unless specifically asked for by the intervener.
11. The translator should be fluent specifically in English and in the language of the non-English–speaking victim.
12. When using the translator, the crisis intervener should speak in short phrases to allow for accurate translation. This is called "chunking," and it takes practice.
13. The translator should translate in short and exact phrases.
14. The translator is not part of the intervention unless specifically needed.
15. Remember: The translator only translates. Nothing more.

Bibliography

APA and MTV (1999, October). Music Television 1999. *Warning signs: A violence prevention guide for youth.* Washington, DC: Author.

Arizona Revised Statue for Privileged Communications, §32-2085 (1965).

Buwa v. Smith, 84-1905 NMB (1986).

Canterbury v. Spense, 464 F. 2d. 772 (D.C. Cir. 1972), cert. den. 93 S.Ct. 560 (1972).

Corsini, R. J. (1981). *Innovative psychotherapies.* New York: Wiley Interscience.

Cutter v. Brownbridge, Cal. Ct. App., 1st Dist. (1986).

Evarts, W. R., Greenstone, J. L., Kirkpatrick, G., and Leviton, S. C. (1984). *Winning through accommodation: The mediator's handbook.* Dubuque, IA: Kendall/Hunt.

Fowler, W. R., and Greenstone, J. L. (1983). Hostage negotiations. In R. Corsini (Ed.), *Encyclopedia of psychology.* New York: Wiley.

Fowler, W. R., and Greenstone, J. L. (1987). Hostage negotiations for police. In R. Corsini (Ed.), *Concise encyclopedia of psychology.* New York: Wiley Interscience.

Fowler, W. R., and Greenstone, J. L. (1989). *Crisis intervention compendium.* Littleton, MA: Copley.

Greenstone, J. L. (1969). Tuning in with our children. *The Single Parent, 1,* 1–5.

Greenstone, J. L. (1970). *The meaning of psychology: A human subject.* Dubuque, IA: Kendall/Hunt.

Greenstone, J. L. (1971). The crisis of discipline. *The Single Parent, 2,* 5–10.

Greenstone, J. L. (1973). Parent's voice . . . child's voice. *The Single Parent, 2,* 5–8.

Greenstone, J. L. (1978). An interdisciplinary approach to marital disputes arbitration: The Dallas plan. *Conciliation Courts Review, 16,* 7–15.

Greenstone, J. L. (1981). Job related stress: Is it killing you? *National Law Journal, 4,* 30–34.

Greenstone, J. L. (1981, July). *Hostage survival.* Paper presented at the meeting of the Plano Amateur Radio Club, Dallas, TX.

Greenstone, J. L. (1981, October). *Crisis intervention: Stress and the police officer.* Paper presented at the meeting of the Society for Police and Criminal Psychology, Baton Rouge, LA.

Greenstone, J. L. (1982, November). *Crisis intervention and what to do if taken hostage.* Paper presented at the meeting of the Protestant Men's Club, Dallas, TX.

Greenstone, J. L. (1983, February 13). The divorce referee. *Dallas Morning News,* "Today" section, p. 20.

Greenstone, J. L. (1984). The crisis at Christmas. *Emotional First Aid: A Journal of Crisis Intervention, 1,* 21–29.

Greenstone, J. L. (1986). The laws of terrorism. *Emotional First Aid: A Journal of Crisis Intervention, 3,* 150–160.

Greenstone, J. L. (1986, June). *Alternatives in dispute resolution: Family and marital mediation.* Paper presented at the meeting of the Fifth International Congress of Family Therapy, Jerusalem, Israel.

Greenstone, J. L. (1992a). The art of negotiating: Tactics and negotiating techniques—the way of the past and the way of the future. *Command: Journal of the Texas Tactical Police Officers Association, 1,* 11–18.

Greenstone, J. L. (1992b). The key to success for hostage negotiations teams: Training, training and more training. *Police Forum, 1,* 3–4.

Greenstone, J. L. (1992, April). *Mediation advocacy: A new concept in the arena of family dispute resolution.* Paper presented at the meeting of the Sixth International Congress on Family Therapy: Divorce and Remarriage Interdisciplinary Issues and Approaches, Jerusalem, Israel.

Greenstone, J. L. (1993a). *Critical Incident Stress Debriefing and Crisis Management.* Austin, Texas: Texas Department of Health.

Greenstone, J. L. (1993b). Violence in the courtroom: Culpability, personal responsibility, sensitivity and justice. The courtroom risk analysis check list. *National Social Science Perspectives Journal, 4*(1), 15–36.

Greenstone, J. L. (1993, Summer). Crisis intervention skills training for police negotiators in the 21st century. Command.

Greenstone, J. L. (1993, October). Violence in the courtroom, part one. *Texas Police Journal,* 17–19.

Greenstone, J. L. (1993, November). Violence in the courtroom, part two. *Texas Police Journal,* 15–18.

Greenstone, J. L. (1993, November/December). Dr. Greenstone's 150 laws for hostage and crisis negotiations. *Police and Security News,* 36–38.

Greenstone, J. L. (1995). Tactics and negotiating techniques (TNT): The way of the past and the way of the future. In M. I. Kurke and E. M. Scrivner (Eds.), *Police psychology into the 21st Century.* Hillsdale, New Jersey: Lawrence Erlbaum Associates.

Greenstone, J. L. (1995, Fall). Police crisis negotiations with AIDS patients and HTLV III/HIV positive persons. *The Journal of Crisis Negotiations.*

Greenstone, J. L. (1998, April-December). The role of tactical emergency medical support in hostage and crisis negotiations. *Prehospital and Disaster Medicine.*

Greenstone, J. L. (2001). *Terrorism and Our Response to It: The New Normalcy.* Booklets prepared for: Fort Worth Police Department; City of Fort Worth; Civil Air Patrol, U.S.A.F.

Greenstone, J. L. (2001, March). Fit to serve: Failure to address stress can cause emotional problems. *Civil Air Patrol News,* 10.

Greenstone, J. L. (2001, September). Fit to serve: Teen suicide. *Civil Air Patrol News,* 5–6.

Greenstone, J. L. (2003, Fall). Terrorism and how we prepare ourselves psychologically to survive it: The new normalcy. *Journal of Police Crisis Negotiations, 3*(2), 91–94.

Greenstone, J. L. (2005). *The elements of police hostage and crisis negotiations: Critical incidents and how to respond to them.* Binghamton, New York: The Haworth Press, Inc.

Greenstone, J. L. (2006, Winter). *The Texas Medical Rangers in the military response of the uniformed medical reserve corps to Hurricane Katrina and Hurricane Rita 2005: The new and tested role of the medical reserve corps in the United States.* Monograph, State Defense Forces Publication Center.

Greenstone, J. L. (2008). *The elements of disaster psychology: Managing Psychosocial Trauma—An integrated approach to force protection and acute care.* Springfield, Illinois: Charles C. Thomas, Publishers.

Greenstone, J. L. (Winter, 2009). A question of inklings that might save your life. *Situational Awareness Newsletter*, 2(3), p. 2.

Greenstone, J. L. (Spring, 2011). Disaster non-preparedness: The orange bag denial. *International Journal of Emergency Mental Health*. Invited Essay. *12*(1), pp. 1–3.

Greenstone, J. L., Dunn, J. M., and Leviton, S. C. (1994). Promotion of mental health for police: The departmental peer counseling programme. In D. R. Trent and C. A. Reed (Eds.), *Promotion of mental health*, 4, 319–340. Aldershot, Hants, England: Avebury, Ashgate Publishing Limited.

Greenstone, J. L., and Leviton, S. C. (1979a). *The crisis intervener's handbook, volume 1.* Dallas, TX: Crisis Management Workshops.

Greenstone, J. L., and Leviton, S. C. (1979b). *Crisis management and intervener survival.* Tulsa, OK: Affective House.

Greenstone, J. L., and Leviton, S. C. (1979c). *Stress reduction: Personal energy management.* Tulsa, OK: Affective House.

Greenstone, J. L., and Leviton, S. C. (1979, July). *Intervention and emergency therapy in marriage and family crises.* Paper presented at the Third International Congress of Family Therapy and Family Life Education, Tel Aviv, Israel.

Greenstone, J. L., and Leviton, S. C. (1980a). *The crisis intervener's handbook, volume 2.* Dallas, TX: Rothschild.

Greenstone, J. L., and Leviton, S. C. (1980b). Crisis management: A basic concern. *Crisis Intervener's Newsletter, 1,* 1–2.

Greenstone, J. L., and Leviton, S. C. (1981a). Crisis management and intervener survival. In R. Corsini (Ed.), *Innovative psychotherapies.* New York: Wiley Interscience.

Greenstone, J. L., and Leviton, S. C. (1981b). *Hotline: Crisis intervention directory.* New York: Facts on file.

Greenstone, J. L., and Leviton, S. C. (1981c). *Training the trainer.* Tulsa, OK: Affective House.

Greenstone, J. L., and Leviton, S. C. (1982). *Crisis intervention: Handbook for interveners.* Dubuque, IA: Kendall/Hunt.

Greenstone, J. L., and Leviton, S. C. (1983a). Crisis intervention. In R. Corsini (Ed.), *Encyclopedia of psychology.* New York: Wiley.

Greenstone, J. L., and Leviton, S. C. (1983b). Executive survival. In R. Corsini (Ed.), *Encyclopedia of psychology.* New York: Wiley.

Greenstone, J. L., and Leviton, S. C. (1983, January). Divorce mediation. *D Magazine,* pp. 3–5.

Greenstone, J. L., and Leviton, S. C. (1983a, March). *Divorce mediation and the attorney.* Paper presented at the meeting of the Family Law Section of the Dallas Bar Association, Dallas, TX.

Greenstone, J. L., and Leviton, S. C. (1983b, March). *Mediation: An alternative to litigation.* Paper presented at the meeting of the Academy of Criminal Justice Sciences, San Antonio, TX.

Greenstone, J. L., and Leviton, S. C. (1983, July). *Mediation: Family dispute resolution.* Paper presented at the meeting of the Fourth International Congress of Family Therapy, Tel Aviv, Israel.

Greenstone, J. L., and Leviton, S. C. (1984, March). *Divorce mediation: The way of the 80's.* Paper presented at the meeting of the Oklahoma Association of Marriage and Family Therapists, Tulsa, OK.

Greenstone, J. L., and Leviton, S. C. (1984a, September). *Crisis intervention in mediation.* Paper presented at the meeting of the National Conference on Peace and Conflict Resolution, St. Louis, MO.

Greenstone, J. L., and Leviton, S. C. (1984b, September). *Management mediation: The police officer's alternative to litigation.* Paper presented at the meeting of the First National Symposium on Police Psychological Services, Quantico, VA.

Greenstone, J. L., and Leviton, S. C. (1984, December). *Crisis management for the mediator.* Paper presented at the meeting of the Second Annual Conference on Problem Solving through Mediation, Albany, NY.

Greenstone, J. L., and Leviton, S. C. (1986a). Intervention procedures. *Emotional First Aid: A Journal of Crisis Intervention, 3,* 100–110.

Greenstone, J. L., and Leviton, S. C. (1986b). Mediation: The police officer's alternative to litigation. In *Psychological services for law enforcement.* Washington, D.C.: U.S. Department of Justice, Federal Bureau of Investigation, U.S. Government Printing Office.

Greenstone, J. L., and Leviton, S. C. (1986c). Referrals: A key to successful crisis intervention. *Emotional First Aid: A Journal of Crisis Intervention, 3,* 75–80.

Greenstone, J. L., and Leviton, S. C. (1986, July). *The dispute mediator as crisis manager: Crisis intervention skills for the mediator in high stress, high risk situations.* Paper presented at the meeting of the Academy of Family Mediators, Minneapolis, MN.

Greenstone, J. L., and Leviton, S. C. (1987a). Crisis intervention. In R. Corsini (Ed.), *Concise encyclopedia of psychology.* New York: Wiley Interscience.

Greenstone, J. L., and Leviton, S. C. (1987b). Crisis management for mediators in high stress, high risk, potentially violent situations. *Mediation Quarterly, 3,* 20–30.

Greenstone, J. L., and Leviton, S. C. (1987c). Executive survival. In R. Corsini (Ed.), *Concise Encyclopedia of Psychology.* New York: Wiley Interscience.

Greenstone, J. L., and Leviton, S. C. (1987, July). *Crisis intervention for mediators in high risk, high stress, potentially violent situations.* Paper presented at the meeting of the Academy of Family Mediators, New York.

Greenstone, J. L., and Leviton, S. C. (1991). *Parents, kids, and war: Information designed to assist parents and children in handling war and its consequences.* Dallas: Leviton & Greenstone.

Greenstone, J. L., and Leviton, S. C. (1992, April). *Crisis management for mediators in high stress, high risk, potentially violent family and divorce mediations.* Paper presented at the meeting of the Sixth International Congress on Family Therapy: Divorce and Remarriage Interdisciplinary Issues and Approaches, Jerusalem, Israel.

Greenstone, J. L., and Leviton, S. C. (1993). *Elements of crisis intervention.* Pacific Grove, CA: Brooks/Cole.

Greenstone, J. L., and Leviton, S. C. (2001, 2d). *Parents, kids and war.* Information to Assist Parents and Children in Handling War and Its Consequences, Booklet, Second Edition. Fort Worth, Texas: Leviton & Greenstone.

Greenstone, J. L., and Leviton, S. C. (2002). *Elements of crisis intervention,* Second Edition. Pacific Grove, CA: Brooks/Cole.

Greenstone, J. L., and Leviton, S. C. (2005, Polish Translation). *Interwencja Kryzysowa.* Gdansk: Gdanskie Wydawnictwo Psychologiczne.

Greenstone, J. L., and Rosenbluh, E. S. (1980). Evolution of the American Academy of Crisis Interveners and the Southwestern Academy of Crisis Interveners. *Crisis Intervener's Newsletter, 1,* 13–14.

Groth, A. N. (1979). *Men who rape.* New York: Plenum Press.

Hales v. Pittman, 118 Ariz. 305, 576 P. 2d. 493 (1978).

Hatton, C. L., Valente, S. M., and Rink, A. (1977). *Suicide: Assessment and intervention.* New York: Appleton-Century-Crofts.

Heilig, S. M. (1970). Training in suicide prevention. *Bulletin of Suicidology*, 6, 6.

Heilig, S. M., Farbernow, N. L., Litman, R. E., and Schneidman, E. S. (1968). The role of the non-professional volunteer in a suicide prevention center. *Community Mental Health Journal*, 4, 287–295.

Hendricks, J., and Greenstone, J. L. (1982, March). *Crisis intervention in criminal justice.* Paper presented at the meeting of the Academy of Criminal Justice Sciences, Louisville, KY.

Holmes, T. H., and Masuda, M. (1973). Life change and illness susceptibility. In B. S. Dohrenwend and B. P. Dohrenwend (Eds.), *Stressful life events: Their nature and effects.* New York: Wiley.

Holmes, T. H., and Rahe, R. H. (1967). The social readjustment rating scale. *Journal of Psychosomatic Research, 11,* 213–218.

Is your kid a killer? (1999). *Psychology Today, 32,* 16.

Jackson, G. (1999). *Disaster mental health: Crisis counseling programs for the rural community.* Washington: U. S. Department of Health and Human Services.

Kelly, G. A. (1961). Suicide: The personal construct point of view. In N. L. Fabernow and E. S. Schneidman (Eds.), *The cry for help.* New York: McGraw-Hill Book Co.

Kempe, C. H., and Helfer, R. E. (1972). *Helping the battered child and his family.* Philadelphia: J. B. Lippincott.

Klein, D., and Lindemann, E. (1961). Preventative intervention in individual and family crisis situations. In G. Caplan (Ed.), *Prevention of mental disorders in children.* New York: Basic Books.

Kubler-Ross, E. (1969). *On death and dying.* London: Macmillan.

Lerner, M. D. (1999). Identifying students "At-Risk" for violent behavior: A checklist of "Early Warning Signs." *A Practical Guide for Crisis Response in Our Schools,* p. 38. (Available from the American Academy of Experts in Traumatic Stress, 368 Veterans Memorial Highway, Commack, New York 11725).

Lester, D. (2001). *Suicide prevention: Resources for the millennium.* Philadelphia, PA: Taylor & Francis.

Leviton, S. C. (1982). National Institute for Crisis Intervention lecture, Louisville, KY.

Leviton, S. C., and Greenstone, J. L. (1980). Intervener survival: Dealing with the givens. *Emotional First Aid: A Journal of Crisis Intervention, 2,* 15–20.

Leviton, S. C., and Greenstone, J. L. (1983a). Conflict mediation. In R. Corsini (Ed.), *Encyclopedia of psychology.* New York: Wiley.

Leviton, S. C., and Greenstone, J. L. (1983b). Intervener survival. In R. Corsini (Ed.), *Encyclopedia of psychology.* New York: Wiley.

Leviton, S. C., and Greenstone, J. L. (1984a). Mediation in potential crisis situations. *Emotional First Aid: A Journal of Crisis Intervention, 1,* 150–155.

Leviton, S. C., and Greenstone, J. L. (1984b). Team intervention. *Emotional First Aid: A Journal of Crisis Intervention, 1,* 20–25.

Leviton, S. C., and Greenstone, J. L. (1987a). Conflict mediation. In R. Corsini (Ed.), *Concise encyclopedia of psychology.* New York: Wiley Interscience.

Leviton, S. C., and Greenstone, J. L. (1987b). Intervener survival. In R. Corsini (Ed.), *Concise encyclopedia of psychology.* New York: Wiley Interscience.

Leviton, S. C., and Greenstone, J. L. (1987c). *Elements of mediation.* Pacific Grove, CA: Brooks/Cole.

Leviton, S. C., and Greenstone, J. L. (2002, Fall). The hostage and crisis negotiator's training laboratory. *Journal of Police Crisis Negotiation,* pp. 21–34.

McDonald v. Clinger, 446 N.Y.S. 2d. 801 (1982).

McIntosh v. Milano, 403 A. 2d. 500 (N.J.S.Ct. 1979).

Mitchell, J. T., (1983). When disaster strikes . . . the critical incident stress debriefing process. *Journal of Emergency Medical Services, 8*(1), 36–39.

Mitchell, J. T., and Everly, G. S. (1996). *Critical incident stress debriefing: An operations manual.* Ellicott City, MD: Chevron Publishing Corp.

Mitchell, J. T., and Resnik, H. L. P. (1981). *Emergency response to crisis.* Bowie, MD: Brady.

Mordock, J. B., Ellis, M. H., and Greenstone, J. L. (1969). The effects of group and individual therapy on sociometric choice of disturbed adolescents. *International Journal of Group Psychotherapy, 4,* 200–210.

New Jersey Revised Statutes, New Jersey Marriage Counseling Act, Annotated § 45: 8B-29 (1969). (Exceptions to Confidentiality).

Pederson, P. A. (1988). *A handbook for developing multicultural awareness.* New York: American Association for Counseling and Development.

People v. District Court, City and County of Denver, 719 P. 2d. 722 (Colo. 1986).

Rodriguez v. Jackson, 118 Ariz. 13, 574 P. 2d. 481 (App. 1978).

Rosenbluh, E. S. (1975). National Institute for Crisis Intervention lecture, Louisville, KY.

Rosenbluh, E. S. (1981). *Emotional first aid.* Louisville, KY: American Academy of Crisis Interveners.

Rosenbluh, E. S. (1986). *Crisis counseling: Emotional first aid.* Dubuque, IA: Kendall/Hunt.

Sard v. Hardy, 291 Md. 432, 379 A. 2d. 1014 (1977).

Selye, H. (1974). *Stress without distress.* Philadelphia: Lippencott.

Slaikeu, K. A. (1984). *Crisis intervention: A handbook for practice and research.* Boston: Allyn & Bacon.

Tarasoff v. Regents of California, 131 Cal. Rptr. 14, 551 P. 2d. 334 (1976).

Whitree v. State of New York, 56 Misc. 2d. 693, 290 N.Y.S. 2s 486 (1968).